GW01057442

Pocke StarterPak
FOR
DUMMIES®

by Brian Underdahl

IDG Books Worldwide, Inc.
An International Data Group Company

Foster City, CA ✦ Chicago, IL ✦ Indianapolis, IN ✦ New York, NY

Pocket PC StarterPak For Dummies®

Published by
IDG Books Worldwide, Inc.
An International Data Group Company
909 Third Avenue
New York, NY 10022
www.idgbooks.com (IDG Books Worldwide Web site)
www.dummies.com (Dummies Press Web site)

Library of Congress Control Number: 00-110788

ISBN: 0-7645-0832-6

Printed in the United States of America

10 9 8 7 6 5 4 3 2 1

1O/QS/QR/QR/IN

Distributed in the United States by IDG Books Worldwide, Inc.

Distributed by CDG Books Canada Inc. for Canada; by Transworld Publishers Limited in the United Kingdom; by IDG Norge Books for Norway; by IDG Sweden Books for Sweden; by IDG Books Australia Publishing Corporation Pty. Ltd. for Australia and New Zealand; by TransQuest Publishers Pte Ltd. for Singapore, Malaysia, Thailand, Indonesia, and Hong Kong; by Gotop Information Inc. for Taiwan; by ICG Muse, Inc. for Japan; by Intersoft for South Africa; by Eyrolles for France; by International Thomson Publishing for Germany, Austria and Switzerland; by Distribuidora Cuspide for Argentina; by LR International for Brazil; by Galileo Libros for Chile; by Ediciones ZETA S.C.R. Ltda. for Peru; by WS Computer Publishing Corporation, Inc., for the Philippines; by Contemporanea de Ediciones for Venezuela; by Express Computer Distributors for the Caribbean and West Indies; by Micronesia Media Distributor, Inc. for Micronesia; by Chips Computadoras S.A. de C.V. for Mexico; by Editorial Norma de Panama S.A. for Panama; by American Bookshops for Finland.

For general information on IDG Books Worldwide's books in the U.S., please call our Consumer Customer Service department at 800-762-2974. For reseller information, including discounts and premium sales, please call our Reseller Customer Service department at 800-434-3422.

For consumer information on foreign language translations, please contact our Customer Service department at 1-800-434-3422, fax 317-572-4002, or e-mail rights@idgbooks.com.

For information on licensing foreign or domestic rights, please phone +1-650-653-7098.

For authorization to photocopy items for corporate, personal, or educational use, please contact Copyright Clearance Center, 222 Rosewood Drive, Danvers, MA 01923, or fax 978-750-4470.

is a registered trademark under exclusive license to IDG Books Worldwide, Inc. from International Data Group, Inc.

About the Author

Brian Underdahl is the well-known, best-selling author of over 50 computer books, including several current titles from IDG Books Worldwide, Inc.: *Opera Web Browser For Dummies, Windows 98 One Step at a Time, Internet Bible Second Edition, Teach Yourself Office 2000, Teach Yourself Windows 2000 Professional,* and *Teach Yourself Windows Me.*

Brian spends most of his time at the keyboard writing about personal computing. When he finds the time, he enjoys taking in the view from the home that he and his wife Darlene built in the mountains 2000 feet above Reno, NV. He tries to find the time to attend Mensa meetings whenever possible, and has become a fairly decent gourmet cook in recent years, too.

Publisher's Acknowledgments

We're proud of this book; please send us your comments through our IDG Books Worldwide Online Registration Form located at http://my2cents.dummies.com.

Some of the people who helped bring this book to market include the following:

Acquisitions, Editorial, and Media Development

Custom Development Editors:
Tamara Castleman, Zoë Wykes

Permissions Editor: Carmen Krikorian

Media Development Specialists:
Brock Bigard, Megan Decraene, Angela Denny

Media Development Assistant:
Marisa Pearman

Product Marketing Manager:
Melisa Duffy

Product Marketing Specialist:
Marcy Assalone

Media Development Manager:
Laura Carpenter

Media Development Supervisor:
Richard Graves

Production

Project Coordinator and Proofreader:
Brian Massey

Layout and Graphics: Beth Brooks, Brian Drumm, Kelly Hardesty

Indexer: Sharon Hilgenberg

General and Administrative

IDG Books Worldwide, Inc.: John Kilcullen, CEO; Bill Barry, President and COO; John Ball, Executive VP, Operations & Administration; John Harris, CFO

IDG Books Technology Publishing Group: Richard Swadley, Senior Vice President and Publisher; Mary Bednarek, Vice President and Publisher; Walter R. Bruce III, Vice President and Publisher; Joseph Wikert, Vice President and Publisher; Mary C. Corder, Editorial Director; Andy Cummings, Publishing Director, General User Group; Barry Pruett, Publishing Director

IDG Books Manufacturing: Ivor Parker, Vice President, Manufacturing

IDG Books Marketing: John Helmus, Assistant Vice President, Director of Marketing

IDG Books Online Management: Brenda McLaughlin, Executive Vice President, Chief Internet Officer; Gary Millrood, Executive Vice President of Business Development, Sales and Marketing

IDG Books Packaging: Marc J. Mikulich, Vice President, Brand Strategy and Research

IDG Books Production for Branded Press: Debbie Stailey, Production Director

IDG Books Sales: Roland Elgey, Senior Vice President, Sales and Marketing; Michael Violano, Vice President, International Sales and Sub Rights

♦

The publisher would like to give special thanks to Patrick J. McGovern, without whom this book would not have been possible.

♦

Table of Contents

Introduction *1*
Why You Need This Book..1
How to Use This Book 1
How This Book Is Organized...................................... 2
Part I: Pocket PCs, the Internet, and Multimedia..........2
Part II: The Part of Tens 2
Icons Used in This Book...2
Where to Go from Here 3

Part I: Pocket PCs, the Internet,
and Multimedia *5*

Chapter 1: The Internet 7
What You Need to Connect...7
Understanding the Pocket PC hardware realities....:....7
Recognizing the service availability realities...............9
Choosing your hardware options 10
Setting up your Pocket PC connection 11
Pocket Internet Explorer Introductions 17
Understanding the Pocket Internet
Explorer screen 18
Setting your general options 19
Choosing your connection options 20
Surfing the connected Web 22
E-mail on Your Pocket PC...23
Setting up your e-mail account 23
Choosing your message options....................................27
Sending and receiving e-mail.......................................28

Chapter 2: Diary of an E-Bookworm 31
Understanding E-Books..31
Downloading E-Books..33
Copying e-books to your Pocket PC 33
Building your e-book library 34
Managing your e-book library.......................................35
Reading an E-Book 36
Navigating an e-book..37
Adding notes and such 39
Listening to Audio Books..40

Chapter 3: That's Pocket PC Entertainment! 43

Playing Music on Your Pocket PC 43
    Transferring music to your Pocket PC.........................43
    Creating a play list..45
    Playing your music 46
    Expanding your Pocket PC's musical capabilities......47
    Finding music online 48
Playing Games on Your Pocket PC.......................................48
Your Pocket PC as Your Digital Camera Companion 50
    Sharing digital images on memory cards 50
    Connecting to your digital camera..............................50
    Editing photos on your Pocket PC...............................51

Part II: The Part of Tens *53*

**Chapter 4: Ten Good Things to Know about
Pocket PCs** **55**

Recognizing What Will and Won't Work
    with Your Pocket PC 55
Moving the Info from a Palm Device into
    Your Pocket PC 57
    Connecting your Palm device with
        your desktop PC..58
    Adding software to connect the Palm device
        to Outlook...58
    Sending data from the Palm device to Outlook 62
    Moving the data to your Pocket PC..............................62
Adding Memory..63
Adding a Modem 63
Connecting to Your Network 64
Powering Your Way to Freedom...65

**Chapter 5: Slightly More than Ten Pocket PC
Applications** **67**

Golfwits by SiscoSoft 67
Developer One Agenda Today v3.01......................................69
Developer One ScreenSnap v5.1 69
Tipster by Ilium Software..70
eWallet by Ilium Software..71
ZIOGolf 72
Bubblets 72
Hearts 72
Windows Media Player...73

PowerToys 73

    Microsoft Power Contacts for Pocket PCs...................73

    Microsoft Today Screen Image Tool for Pocket PCs ..74

    Windows Media Skin Chooser for Pocket PCs 74

ActiveSync Extras 74

    Microsoft Pocket Streets..74

    Microsoft Transcriber 75

BSQUARE..76

    BSQUARE bUseful Utilities Pak 76

    BSQUARE bFax 5.0 77

    BSQUARE Messenger 1.1 78

Index *79*

CD Installation *83*

Introduction

· ·

*P*ocket PCs are amazing little devices. Who knew such a
small machine could do so much? Who knew a Pocket PC
could make your life so much easier? Who knew a Pocket PC
could come with so many headaches?

Like all gadgets designed to make your life more relaxed and
organized, a Pocket PC isn't much good until you understand
how to make it do all the things you've been told it can do.
That's where this book comes in. Not only do I tell you how
to make your Pocket PC do all those useful tasks you bought it
for, but I also show you several things that make your Pocket
PC even cooler than you thought.

Why You Need This Book

This book is bursting at the binding with all sorts of useful tid-
bits for a Pocket PC owner. And because you own a Pocket PC,
I'm assuming you need, or at least want, this information. I
recognize that you're a busy person. If you weren't, you probably wouldn't have invested in this terrific machine. So I'm
here to let you in on some Pocket PC tricks-of-the-trade —
quickly! This book will help you maximize your time and
energy, and the bonus CD in the back will add a little more
"fun and carefree" to your life.

How to Use This Book

Use this book to get the information you need. Your book
club won't know if you only read the first chapter, and neither
will your mother. And, you can skip to the end without spoil-
ing the ending. If you're the kind of person who always reads
a book cover to cover, then keep on reading until you hit the
index. But if you're the sort of person who firmly operates
on a need-to-know basis, then look at the Table of Contents
or the index, find what you need, and then put the book away.

How This Book Is Organized

This book is organized into two logical parts, both of which are designed to enhance your Pocket PC experience.

Part I: Pocket PCs, the Internet, and Multimedia

This part shows you how to take full advantage of some nifty Pocket PC features. Chapter 1 delves into accessing the Internet via your Pocket PC and using e-mail — bet you didn't know you had a portable mailbox with a 24-hour post office, did you? Chapter 2 talks about e-books. Pocket PCs put a library at your fingertips, and you'll never, ever again disturb the person who sleeps next to you when you're up until 3 a.m. finishing the latest thriller. Finally, Chapter 3 explores other fun things you can do with your Pocket PC, including playing music and games on your Pocket PC and using your Pocket PC as a companion to your digital camera.

Part II: The Part of Tens

A standard feature in all *For Dummies* books, each Part of Tens chapter offers you ten (or thereabouts) nuggets of tasty information for your intellectual palate. Chapter 4 lets you in on some good things to know about your Pocket PC; Chapter 5 explains each of the Pocket PC applications that are on the CD in the back of this book, itching to be downloaded to your Pocket PC.

Icons Used in This Book

After you read a while, you're bound to notice some little pictures off to the side of a paragraph or attached to the top of a sidebar. These pictures are *icons*, and they're meant to point out specific information:

You'll see this icon anytime I have a tip (hence the word "tip" on the icon) to share that will make your Pocket PC run more smoothly, intuitively, or efficiently.

 This icon points out things that will make your life easier if you remember them. (By the way, if you think you'll forget to remember a Remember icon, you can always use a sticky note or a bookmark to help.)

 I don't know about you, but when I see a picture of a bomb, I'm pretty sure that things can't be good. Disregard the advice in paragraphs attatched to this icon at your own risk.

 If you're one of those people who can't get enough information about the why and how of things, then you'll enjoy the information in paragraphs marked with this icon. If, on the other hand, all you want to do is make the darn thing do what it's supposed to do, skip these paragraphs entirely.

Where to Go from Here

Where you go from here depends on what you want to do with your Pocket PC. If you can't wait to try some of the applications provided on the CD at the back of the book, then go straight to your computer and open up Chapter 5. If you want to be the first on your block to read *War and Peace* on a Pocket PC, then head to Chapter 2. If you want even more information, check out *Pocket PCs For Dummies*, published by IDG Books Worldwide, Inc. If you've worn yourself out reading the introduction, use the book as a pillow and go take a nap. Your book, your call, your rules.

Part I
Pocket PCs, the Internet, and Multimedia

The 5th Wave   By Rich Tennant

It's an e-mail from my mother. She wants me to know how happy she is for us.

In this part . . .

This part lets you in on some very practical aspects of Pocket PC ownership. You know, things like using your Pocket PC for Internet access and e-mail, and how to move information from a Palm device to your Pocket PC. Then I move on to the really important stuff — e-books, games, and music!

Chapter 1

The Internet

In This Chapter
▶ Connecting to the Internet
▶ Understanding Pocket Internet Explorer and your Pocket PC
▶ Using your Pocket PC for e-mail

*I*n the past five or so years the Internet has gone from being primarily a toy for college students to being one of the most important means of communication worldwide. These days, even your local used-car dealer is likely to have an Internet site in its name. And no wonder — the Internet really has influenced society in ways no one could have imagined. This chapter examines how the Internet and your Pocket PC work together.

What You Need to Connect

Sorry to tell you this, but your Pocket PC needs help. That is, your Pocket PC needs some help in order to be able to connect to the Internet. Pocket PCs don't come with the hardware necessary to connect directly to the Internet. For that you're going to have to get some extra pieces.

Understanding the Pocket PC hardware realities

If being able to connect your Pocket PC to the Internet is such a big deal, why don't Pocket PCs simply include the necessary pieces to make the connection? After all, don't the Pocket PC manufacturers realize you want to be able to connect?

Unfortunately, this problem is more complex than it seems. When connecting a Pocket PC to the Internet, a perfect solution for me may not work at all for you. Indeed, a solution that works perfectly for you in some cases may be totally useless in others. Here are some reasons why:

- ✔ **The most common type of expansion slot on Pocket PCs is the CF slot:** Currently you can get a *wired modem* — a modem that plugs into a standard phone line, or a *digital phone card* that plugs into a digital cell phone, to fit the CF slot.

  CF slots come in two sizes that are called *Type 1* and *Type 2*. The only really important difference between these two is the thickness of the cards that will fit into the slot. All Type 1 cards will fit into any Type 2 slot, but Type 2 cards are too thick to fit Type 1 slots. Currently the CF slot communication options all are Type 1 size and will fit any CF slot. Still, check to make sure that you're getting a card that will fit your Pocket PC before you plunk down your money.

- ✔ **PC Card slots are much larger than CF slots:** Currently the only Pocket PC that can use a PC Card device is the Compaq iPAQ H3650, and then only if you add the PC Card Expansion Adapter sleeve (Compaq part number 170338-B21).

- ✔ **Digital phone cards are specific to certain brands and models of cell phones:** You must get the correct one for your phone.

- ✔ **CF slot devices can be used in PC Card slots by using an inexpensive adapter:** However, you can't go in the opposite direction.

So, bottom line: You need at least a CF slot to connect your Pocket PC to the Internet. You also need a modem or cell phone adapter, and you need equipment that's compatible with your Pocket PC and with whatever Internet Service Provider (ISP) you choose to use.

Recognizing the service availability realities

Before you get your hopes set on one type of Internet connection option for your Pocket PC, you also must consider another very important factor. Namely, can you even use the hardware in the area where you are? Here are some very important considerations:

- ✔ **Some phone jacks can kill your modem:** You probably take it for granted that you can plug a regular wired modem into most regular phone jacks and make a connection. That belief is mostly true, but not always. *Digital* phone lines — like many businesses use — produce voltages that will fry your modem. So if you want to use your wired modem, you may not be able to do so from your office or hotel room unless you can plug into an *analog* phone line. Definitely check before plugging in.

- ✔ **Wireless modems typically require *CDPD* (Cellular Digital Packet Data) service:** Unfortunately, CDPD coverage isn't available in all areas. Large metropolitan areas generally have good coverage, but overall, the coverage isn't widespread enough yet that you can take it for granted.

- ✔ **Digital phone cards require a digital phone and digital service:** If your cell phone is analog, you can't use a digital phone card. If your cell phone is digital, but the signal in your area is only analog, you can't connect with a digital phone card.

- ✔ **Wireless connections today are much slower than wired ones:** In fact, a typical wireless connection speed is 14.4 kbps or even slower. Most wired modems are 56K modems.

- ✔ **Wireless modems typically require a separate service contract from your cell phone contract:** Separate service can get quite expensive — especially when you consider that a digital phone card typically allows you to connect with little or no extra charge other than your airtime. If you have a cell phone contract that leaves you with quite a bit of unused airtime each month, the difference can be considerable.

Choosing your hardware options

After you decide on the type of service you want to use to connect your Pocket PC to the Internet, you need to pick out the hardware.

By picking the type of service first, you won't waste time buying the wrong equipment. You may want to consider more than one option. For example, you may want to buy a wired modem so you'll have the fastest and cheapest service when a telephone line is available, and one of the wireless options for when you're on the go.

CF wired modems

Compact Flash (CF) wired modems may not be the sexiest way to connect your Pocket PC to the Internet, but they offer some real advantages over any other option. Not only are CF wired modems inexpensive and fast, but they also let you connect through your regular Internet account that you use on your desktop PC. But even if you were to set up a separate Internet account just for your Pocket PC, unlimited access is generally quite reasonable — or even free, in some cases.

CF digital phone cards

If you already have a digital cell phone, a CF digital phone card may be available for your phone. These phone cards plug into your Pocket PC and your cell phone, and allow you to connect to the Internet wherever a digital cell phone signal is available.

Wireless modems

If your Pocket PC supports it, a PC Card wireless modem is about the coolest way to connect your Pocket PC to the Internet. With a PC Card wireless modem, only a small antenna sticks out from your Pocket PC, and you can concentrate on browsing rather than worrying about wires. Currently the only Pocket PC that can use a PC Card wireless modem is the Compaq iPAQ H3650.

Minstrel wireless modems

While writing this book, I've been informed about another wireless modem — the Minstrel 540 from Novatel Wireless — that will work with the HP Jornada 540 series of Pocket PCs. The Minstrel 540 will clip onto the back of the Jornada and provide the same type of service as a PC Card wireless modem. The Minstrel 540 should be released by the time you read this, so if you use an HP Jornada 540 series Pocket PC, go to www.novatelwireless.com for more details.

Setting up your Pocket PC connection

After you get the hardware and arrange for any service that may be required, you can set up the connection on your Pocket PC so that you can actually begin browsing the Internet and sending e-mail.

You can only have one active connection at a time. If your Pocket PC is sitting in the synchronization cradle, be sure to remove it from the cradle before you want to use any other type of connection, such as a modem.

Setting up a wired modem connection

Setting up your wired modem to work with your Pocket PC will probably seem fairly familiar — especially if you've ever added a modem to your desktop PC. Your Pocket PC automatically recognizes your new modem, so all you have to do is set up the connection. Make sure that you push the modem fully into the expansion slot before you begin.

Here's the step-by-step procedure:

1. **Choose Start⇨Settings, and then tap the Connections tab as shown in Figure 1-1.**

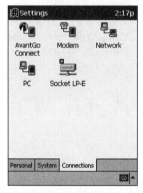

Figure 1-1: Every new connection begins on the Connections tab.

2. **Tap Modem to open the Modem Connections screen, shown in Figure 1-2.**

This screen lists all of the Internet connections you've set up on your Pocket PC — no matter which type of modem you're using. If you have more than one ISP, you may end up with several different connections, as shown in the figure.

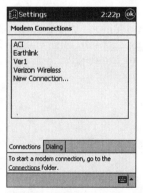

Figure 1-2: Use this screen to add a new connection or to edit an existing one.

3. Tap New Connection to begin adding a new connection.

Doing so displays the Make New Connection screen shown in Figure 1-3.

Figure 1-3: You're finally ready to begin configuring your new connection.

4. Enter a descriptive name for this connection in the first box near the top of the screen.

Make this name distinctive enough so you can tell your different connections apart when you're ready to connect.

5. Choose which modem you want to use from the Select a Modem list.

If you have more than one type of modem, you'll see several options in this box.

6. Select 57600 from the Baud Rate list box.

All wired Pocket PC modems use this setting.

7. Click the Advanced button, and then tap the TCP/IP tab as shown in Figure 1-4.

Figure 1-4: Next you need to adjust your TCP/IP settings.

8. **Remove the check from the Use IP Header Compression checkbox.**

   If you check this box, you may have a bit more difficulty connecting.

9. **If your ISP has specified DNS addresses for you to use, click the Name Servers tab; select the Use Specific Server Address option button, and then enter the addresses in the first two address boxes.**

   Figure 1-5 shows this tab after the Earthlink DNS addresses have been entered.

Figure 1-5: Use these settings if your ISP specifies specific DNS addresses.

10. **Click OK, and then click Next to continue.**

11. **Type the correct dial-up number for your ISP, as shown in Figure 1-6.**

    If you're setting up a connection to use while you're traveling, be sure to enter the correct area code (and country code if you'll be in another country).

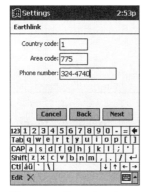

Figure 1-6: Enter the phone number your modem needs to call in order to reach the Internet.

12. **Click Next, and then click Finish.**

    Your connection setup is nearly complete, but you can't do the final setup until you use the connection the first time.

13. **Choose Start⇨Programs, and then tap the Connections folder to open the folder.**

14. **Tap the icon for the new connection you just created to open the Connect To screen (shown in Figure 1-7).**

Figure 1-7: Enter your user name and password before you try to connect.

15. **Add your user name and password to the top two boxes.**

    You probably don't need to fill in the *Domain* box unless your ISP specifically tells you to do so.

16. **Decide whether you want to have your Pocket PC save your password so you don't have to enter it each time you want to connect.**

    Leaving the Save Password checkbox empty provides a bit more security, but means that you'll always have to enter your password to connect.

17. **Tap the Connect button and wait while your Pocket PC attempts to connect to the Internet.**

Setting up a digital phone card connection

Setting up a digital phone card connection is much like setting up a wired modem connection with a few important differences:

✔ **Leave the 19200 selection alone in the Baud Rate list box:** Digital phone cards typically connect at 14400, so you don't need to change this setting.

✔ **If you're using your cell service provider's Internet service, you may enter something like #777 — the access number for the Verizon Wireless Internet access service.**

✔ **Remove the check from the Wait for Dial Tone Before Dialing checkbox:** Because cell phones don't use a dial tone, you need to tell your Pocket PC to just go ahead and dial without waiting for the dial tone.

✔ **If you're using your cell service provider's Internet access, you'll probably use a generic user name and password:** For example, Verizon Wireless has all users enter **qnc** (make certain you use lowercase letters) for both the user name and the password.

Setting up a wireless modem connection

Wireless modems are pretty much a cross between a modem and a cell phone. As such, setting up the connection is quite similar to setting up a wired modem connection with a few small differences thrown in just to keep things interesting.

One of the most important differences to keep in mind with a wireless modem connection is simply that the wireless modem is always set up as a separate account with the CDPD service provider. The wireless modem does not use your cell phone's account or airtime.

Pocket Internet Explorer Introductions

Pocket Internet Explorer is a *Web browser* (a program that displays Web pages more or less about the way the Web page designer intended) designed for the Pocket PC's small screen. On your desktop PC you probably use Internet Explorer, Netscape Communicator, or Opera as your Web browser, but none of those is able to run on a Pocket PC. Pocket Internet Explorer, of course, is similar to Internet Explorer, but it's different, too.

Understanding the Pocket Internet Explorer screen

Figure 1-8 shows the Pocket Internet Explorer screen that you'll probably see the first time you open Pocket Internet Explorer. You don't need to be connected to the Internet to see this screen, which is stored right on your Pocket PC. In fact, you don't need to connect until you actually want to visit a Web site.

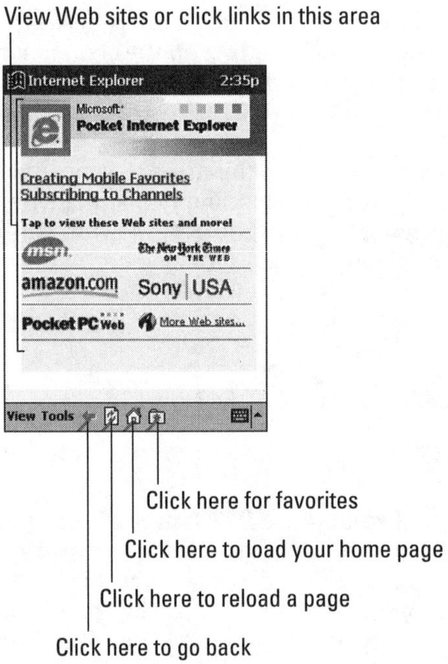
View Web sites or click links in this area
Internet Explorer 2:35p
Microsoft
Pocket Internet Explorer
Creating Mobile Favorites
Subscribing to Channels
Tap to view these Web sites and more!
amazon.com
Sony USA
Pocket PC Web
More Web sites...
View Tools
Click here for favorites
Click here to load your home page
Click here to reload a page
Click here to go back

Figure 1-8: Pocket Internet Explorer enables you to surf the Web on your Pocket PC.

Right off the bat you've probably noticed that the Pocket Internet Explorer screen looks quite a bit different from any other Web browser you've used in the past. For one thing, far fewer things like buttons and toolbars clutter up the screen. For another, because Pocket Internet Explorer has far less room to waste, Web pages tend to have a more compact appearance with far less empty space between the various bits and pieces.

Even with a more compact view of Web pages you still need to be able to move around. Fortunately you don't need to acquire any new skills to navigate Web pages by using Pocket Internet Explorer. You can still click a link to load a different Web page by tapping the link with your stylus. You can still use the address bar to enter a URL — although you will have to use View⇨Address Bar to display the address bar first because it's normally hidden to give you more browsing room. And you can still scroll to other areas on a Web page by using the scroll bars that appear when the Web page is too large for a single screen.

Setting your general options

Pocket Internet Explorer has a number of options that you can set to control how the program works. You may want to have a quick look at these options before you actually begin browsing with Pocket Internet Explorer so you can be sure that you understand exactly what will work the best for you.

To begin setting the Pocket Internet Explorer options, choose Tools⇨Options on the Pocket Internet Explorer menu bar to display the General tab shown in Figure 1-9.

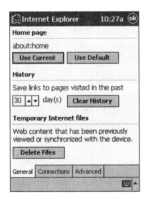

Figure 1-9: This page shows a few of the Pocket Internet Explorer options you can control.

Here's a brief explanation of the options on the General tab:

- ✔ **The Home page buttons enable you to choose a specific Web page to view whenever you open Pocket Internet Explorer:** Select Use Current if you're viewing a Web page that you want as your home page, or Use Default to return to the Web page shown in Figure 1-8. Choose a Web page that's always available, and since your Pocket PC isn't likely to be connected to the Internet all the time, I suggest a Web page that is stored on your Pocket PC. Because the default Web page is stored on your Pocket PC, you don't need to connect in order to view the page. If you choose an online Web page, Pocket Internet Explorer won't be able to load the page unless your Pocket PC is connected.

- ✔ **The History options enable you to control how long Pocket Internet Explorer maintains a record of your browsing:** The longer links remain in the history list, the more likely you'll be able to find the link when you want to return to a page but can't quite remember the URL. Of course, like most everything else on your Pocket PC, use moderation in choosing how long to keep things in the history because everything you store eats up some memory.

- ✔ **The Delete Files button in the Temporary Internet files section is used to remove any Web pages and their associated files from temporary storage:** These files are stored so that you can more quickly reload a Web page that you've visited recently.

If you're really running low on memory, click the Clear History button and the Delete Files button. You typically won't free up very much room this way, but it may be enough to temporarily solve the problem.

Choosing your connection options

Next you get to choose how Pocket Internet Explorer connects to the Internet. Click the Connections tab, as shown in Figure 1-10, to select these options.

Figure 1-10: Set up Pocket Internet Explorer's connection options on this page.

Here's what you need to know about the connection options:

✔ **The Type box enables you to specify which connection to use:** This selection isn't too important unless you also select the next option because you can always open the connection you prefer before you open Pocket Internet Explorer.

✔ **If you select the Access Remote Content Automatically option, Pocket Internet Explorer attempts to open the connection whenever it needs to load something from the Internet:** Although seemingly harmless, choosing to use this option can quickly become very expensive if you use a wireless Internet connection and pay for your airtime. Instead, take the extra time to open your Internet connection manually whenever you want to surf the Web.

✔ **If you do use a proxy you'll need to know the settings that work with your proxy server in order to connect:** You're pretty unlikely to need to use any of the settings in the Proxy section because most people don't use a *proxy* — a special computer that essentially filters incoming and outgoing Internet traffic — to access the Web.

Surfing the connected Web

Now you're ready to see what Web browsing on a Pocket PC is really like.

To begin having some fun on the Web, first open your Internet connection. In case you don't remember how, here's a quick refresher:

1. **Choose Start⇨Programs.**

2. **Tap the Connections folder, and then tap the Internet connection you want to use.**

3. **Type the password and tap Connect (if you haven't already set up your Pocket PC to save your password).**

Web sites are all identified by their unique address — their _URL_. If you want to view the IDG Books Worldwide, Inc. Web site, for example, your can enter the address `www.idgbooks.com` and your Web browser finds and loads the page you requested.

To display the Pocket Internet Explorer address bar, choose View⇨Address Bar from the menu bar. This option is a _toggle_, so you use the same command a second time to make the address bar go away again.

As you surf the Web you're bound to come across Web pages that you'd like to share with someone else. Pocket Internet Explorer provides a very easy way to do so by allowing you to send the URL in an e-mail message. The recipient can then click the link and view the page.

To send a Web page link to someone, do the following:

1. **Make certain that you're viewing the page you want to send.**

2. **Choose Tools⇨Send Link via E-mail.**

3. **Address your message and include an explanation so the recipient knows why you're sending the link.**

Following links to make your way home

Almost all Web pages include *links* that you can follow to visit other Web pages. It is, in fact, those links that inspired the name "Web" in the first place. The Web really is an endless web of links that lead here and there. Links are also one of the most fun things about the Web. You never know where you'll eventually end up if you start following interesting looking links.

After you follow a bunch of interesting looking links, you may find yourself yearning to return to the sanity of home — your *home page*, that is. In that case, just click the little house symbol on the Pocket Internet Explorer menu bar. Pocket Internet Explorer reloads your home page. Too bad it can't also bring you a plate of homemade chocolate chip cookies at the same time.

E-mail on Your Pocket PC

E-mail has become an integral part of life for most PC users, so being able to use your Pocket PC for e-mail probably really comes in handy for you.

Setting up your e-mail account

E-mail messages move over the Internet much like letters travel through the postal system, albeit more quickly. First, all e-mail messages need to be sent to a specific, unique address. In addition, e-mail messages travel through *mail servers* — the electronic equivalent of post offices. Just as you have to establish your street address with the post office, you also have to establish your e-mail address with a mail server.

If you set up your Pocket PC to use the same e-mail account as your desktop PC, you can more easily share e-mail between the two. To set up your e-mail account on your Pocket PC, follow these steps:

1. **Choose Start⇨Inbox, and then tap Services⇨New Service on the Inbox menu bar to display the Service Name screen, shown in Figure 1-11.**

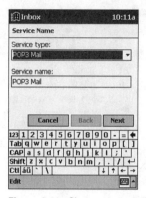

Figure 1-11: Choose your mail server type and add a name if you like.

2. **Select the type of mail server from the drop-down Service Type box.**

   Most mail servers use POP3 protocols, but IMAP4 is becoming more popular.

3. **Enter a name for this mail server if you like.**

   Entering a name is optional, but I recommend that you do — especially if you use more than one mail service — so you can tell them apart.

4. **Click Next to continue and to display the screen shown in Figure 1-12.**

Figure 1-12: Here you enter the information necessary to access your mail server.

5. **Select the type of Internet connection you're going to use with your Pocket PC.**

6. **Enter the server name in the Server box.**

   If your ISP has both an incoming and an outgoing mail server, enter the incoming mail server.

7. **Enter your user name and your password if you want your Pocket PC to be able to send and receive e-mail automatically.**

   If you either skip the password or don't check the Save Password option, you have to enter the information manually each time you want to access the mail server.

8. **Click Next to display the screen shown in Figure 1-13.**

   In most cases you won't enter anything into the top box. The Domain setting primarily applies if you send and receive e-mail through a Windows NT network mail server.

Figure 1-13: Use this screen to enter information on outgoing mail.

9. **If your ISP has an outgoing mail server, enter the server's name in the middle box.**

10. **Enter your e-mail address in the last box and click Next to display the screen shown in Figure 1-14.**

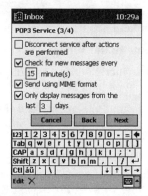

Figure 1-14: Here you control how Pocket Inbox handles mail.

11. **Select the mail service settings that work best for you.**

For example, I suggest you select Disconnect Service After Actions Are Performed to make certain your Pocket PC disconnects from the Internet after it sends and receives your messages.

12. **Click Next to display the final screen as shown in Figure 1-15.**

Figure 1-15: Decide how much of each message to download to your Pocket PC.

13. **Choose the options to control how much of each message you want to download.**

    If you're using your Pocket PC as a companion to a desktop PC, go ahead and accept the default settings shown in the preceding figure. That way, you can identify and respond to urgent messages from your Pocket PC, while your desktop PC downloads all messages completely — including any attachments.

14. **Tap Finish to complete the setup.**

Choosing your message options

Before you begin using a new mail service, always at least review the message options that are selected for the mail service. That way you can be certain that Pocket Inbox is handling mail the way you prefer. To check the message options, choose Tools➪Options from the Pocket Inbox menu bar, and then click the Message tab as shown in Figure 1-16.

Figure 1-16: Set the message options the way you want them.

Here's a brief description of these options:

✔ **Use When Replying, Include Body to include the original message when you send a reply to someone:** If you don't select this option, people will have difficulty remembering which message you're replying to.

When you include the original message in your reply, cut down the clutter by deleting those parts of the original that aren't necessary to convey the message. If you include the body text in replies, make certain that you select both the Indent and Add Leading Character boxes: Doing so allows the the recipient to more easily recognize the text to which you're replying. Don't try to get fancy with the leading character, either. Everyone recognizes the greater than (>) symbol as signifying a reply. If you decide to use a different character, you'll only confuse people.

✔ **Use Keep Copy of Sent Mail in Sent Folder to keep a record of messages you send:** You may be tempted to try and save storage space by not selecting this option, but then you won't have any way to determine whether you've actually sent a message or simply thought you should and then forgot.

✔ **Select an option for After Moving/Deleting a Message to determine how you want Pocket Inbox to respond when you finish with a message:** Experiment with the three possibilities to see which best fits your way of working.

✔ **Use the Empty Deleted Items selections to determine what Pocket Inbox should do with messages you delete.**

Sending and receiving e-mail

E-mail is really one of the great inventions of the computing age. E-mail allows you to send a quick message at any time and have that message delivered almost instantly. But unlike other forms of communication, e-mail is also cheap and has the ability to bridge time differences between people anywhere in the world. You can send a message at your convenience to your friend half way around the world, and you don't have to worry about waking her with an expensive phone call.

Creating a message

Creating an e-mail message is a very simple process: Write a quick note, add the recipient's address, and add a subject line. To create an e-mail message, tap New on the Pocket Inbox menu bar, which opens a message form like the one I'm using in Figure 1-17.

Figure 1-17: Enter your e-mail message as I'm doing here.

Enter the recipient's name or e-mail address in the To field. You can click on To if you want to select the message recipients from your address list. If you click To, you see only those people in your address list who have e-mail addresses.

Use the Subj: line to briefly describe your message. Coming up with a good subject line can be a real art, because you want to distill your meaning down into just a few words. The message recipient needs to be able to grasp the message's importance from seeing the first few words of the subject line — long subject lines probably won't display completely in an Inbox.

When you finish composing your message, click the Send button to place the message into your Outbox folder. Items in the Outbox folder go out the next time you contact the mail server.

Sending and receiving messages

If you configured Pocket Inbox to automatically send and receive e-mail, you don't have to do anything special to send the messages from your Outbox. Those messages go out and any new messages are received as soon as your Pocket PC connects to the mail server.

You can, however, tell your Pocket PC to send and receive messages immediately by clicking the Send/Receive button (the button with two envelopes at the right side of the Inbox menu bar). Depending on your settings, you may need to connect to the Internet manually, and you may need to enter your mail server user name and password.

Chapter 2

Diary of an E-Bookworm

● ●

In This Chapter

▶ Getting to know e-books

▶ Finding your e-books

▶ Reading e-books

▶ Listening to audio books

● ●

*A*nyone who uses a Pocket PC knows that having a computer that fits easily into your shirt pocket opens a whole new range of possibilities. The *e-book* represents a great example of just how much these new ideas can change the way you do ordinary things. In this case, that ordinary thing is something you're doing right now in the old traditional way — reading a book. If this were an e-book, you wouldn't be looking at ink printed on paper, but rather at words on your Pocket PC's screen.

Understanding E-Books

E-books are different from the plain old text you've been seeing since you started using computers in several ways:

  ✔ **A Pocket PC is about the size of a paperback book, so you can easily hold your Pocket PC in your hand while you read an e-book:** Consequently, reading an e-book is far more like reading a "real" book than like reading text on a computer screen.

  ✔ **The Microsoft Reader program you use to read e-books allows you to search, bookmark, and even annotate e-books:** You can even ask for the definition of unfamiliar words as you're reading.

✔ **Many popular books — including current best sellers — are available as e-books, but not as plain text files:** The e-book format allows publishers to control the distribution of titles so that both the authors and publishers can earn the money they deserve from their efforts.

✔ **A Pocket PC screen is backlit:** You can read an e-book in the dark without trying to find a flashlight that doesn't have dead batteries.

E-books are stored in a highly compressed format that greatly reduces the amount of storage space you need. This format also allows publishers to control who can read an e-book. Because of the special format, you need a special program to read e-books. On your Pocket PC that program is Microsoft Reader.

The E-Book Connections Web site, `www.ebookconnections. com/ReadersPrimer`, contains an excellent introduction to the world of e-books. At this site, shown in Figure 2-1, you can find up-to-date information on just about anything you may want to know about e-books.

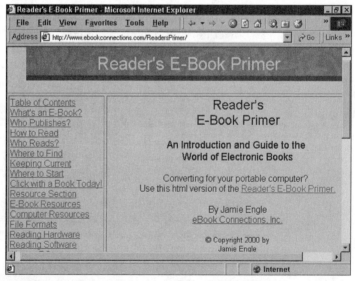

Figure 2-1: Visit the Reader's E-Book Primer Web site to get the latest info on e-books.

Downloading E-Books

In order to read an e-book on your Pocket PC, you first have to get those e-books into your Pocket PC. The process is similar to copying other files to your Pocket PC, with a few differences.

Copying e-books to your Pocket PC

The first e-books you're likely to try out are the free samples included on the ActiveSync CD-ROM. You may as well see whether you like reading e-books on your Pocket PC before you spend time and money on other e-books, right?

To copy any of the e-books to your Pocket PC, follow these steps:

1. **Make sure that your Pocket PC is connected to your desktop PC, and open ActiveSync if it isn't already open.**

2. **Click the Explore button in ActiveSync.**

3. **Open Windows Explorer on your desktop PC and navigate to the folder where the e-book files are located.**

   On the ActiveSync CD-ROM look in the \Extras\ MS Reader\books folder. (If you read and follow the advice in the "For your eyes read-only" sidebar, then you may want to copy the files to a folder on your hard drive.)

4. **Select the files you want to copy in Windows Explorer, and then drag-and-drop them into the My Documents folder that is open in the ActiveSync Explore window.**

 Be selective about which e-book files you copy to your Pocket PC. Unless you've added a memory storage card and are copying the files to the storage card, the 7.24 MB of e-book files on the ActiveSync CD-ROM probably won't all fit in your available storage memory at the same time.

For your eyes read-only

Files you copy directly from a CD-ROM always have their *read-only* file attribute set. This setting doesn't present any problems when you want to read e-books on your Pocket PC, but it does produce a cryptic error message when you later decide to free up some storage space on your Pocket PC. To prevent this problem, do the following:

1. **Copy the e-book files from the CD-ROM to your desktop PC's hard drive.**

2. **Right-click the copied files and choose Properties.**

3. **Remove the check from the Read-only checkbox, and then click OK.**

Now you can copy the files from your hard drive to your Pocket PC and you won't have any problem when you later want to delete an e-book.

Building your e-book library

You aren't limited to the selection of e-books from the ActiveSync CD-ROM, of course. You can also download e-books from a number of different Web sites. Figure 2-2 shows one such site, the eBook Directory, www.ebookdirectory.com.

The E-Book Connection Web site (www.ebookconnections.com/) offers links to many more e-book vendors. Some sites offer a selection of free e-books in addition to titles you can purchase.

Unfortunately, many things fit loosely into the definition of e-books. Most things called "e-books" aren't designed to be read on your Pocket PC. When you download e-books, make certain that you're downloading files that are specified as being Microsoft Reader-compatible files. Otherwise you'll be wasting your time (and maybe money) downloading files you can't use on your Pocket PC.

Figure 2-2: You can download e-books from many sites, including this one.

Managing your e-book library

Managing your e-book collection is easy. The main things you need to do are control where your e-books reside on your Pocket PC, and delete e-books you no longer need to free up space for other uses. Here are a few points to consider:

✓ **A memory storage card is an excellent place to store your e-books:** You don't need any other accessories (such as modems) to read e-books, so you can keep your entire e-book collection on a memory storage card that you pop in whenever you want to view your library. Remember to place the e-book files in the My Documents folder on the memory storage card.

✓ **You may encounter a cryptic error message if you try to delete an e-book by using tap-and-hold and selecting Delete from within Reader:** If you do, then the file is probably set to read-only, which means you can't delete it from within Reader.

✔ **You can use the File Explorer on your Pocket PC to delete or move files:** Even so, clicking the Explore button in ActiveSync on your desktop PC and then managing those files from your desktop PC is usually easier.

✔ **The Encarta Pocket Dictionary file eats lots of storage space on your Pocket PC:** In fact, installing this e-book burns up almost 2.5 MB of memory. Considering how little memory is available on most Pocket PCs, you can probably live without this memory hog.

Reading an E-Book

Some people build up big collections of fancy-looking books but never read a single one of them. You'll probably be far more practical about your e-book collection — especially since e-books just don't have the same panache as a library full of leather-bound law books.

To open an e-book, follow these steps:

1. **Choose Start⇨Programs.**

2. **Tap Microsoft Reader to open the library, as shown in Figure 2-3.**

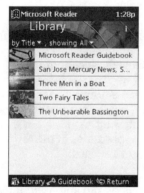

Figure 2-3: The library shows all of the e-books that are currently on your Pocket PC.

3. Tap a book title to open that book.

Figure 2-4 shows that I've opened some Hans Christian Andersen fairly tales.

Figure 2-4: After you open an e-book, you're ready to begin reading.

Navigating an e-book

Reading an e-book is most definitely different from reading a bound-paper book or even from reading a text document on your desktop PC. For one thing, how do you flip the pages?

As you can see in Figure 2-4, the title page of each e-book contains several options you can tap to navigate your way through the book. To begin at the beginning, you tap First Page (score one for pointing out the obvious!). The Reader also keeps track of how far you've read and the last page you were viewing — so you don't have to try and dog-ear any of the pages.

After you begin reading, the Reader shows several things near the top of each page, as shown in Figure 2-5, and you can use these to navigate your way through the book:

✔ **The down arrow just to the right of the book title pops up a menu:** You can use this menu to return to the beginning, open your list of annotations, view the guidebook, open the library, change the view settings, or return to the last page you were viewing.

✔ **The left arrow returns you to the next lower-numbered page:** This page may not be the last one you were reading if you jumped to a page from an annotation or from the index.

✔ **The right arrow displays the next higher-numbered page:** The current page number appears between the two page navigation arrows.

Figure 2-5: You can navigate through an e-book by using the arrows near the top of the page.

Tapping the right or left arrow to move through the pages soon gets tedious. That's why all Pocket PCs offer alternative methods for navigating the pages of an e-book. Here's what you find on your Pocket PC:

✔ **On HP Jornada 540-series Pocket PCs, use the rocker switch on the left side of the Pocket PC to page through the book:** Each time you flick the switch up or down you move one page backward or forward through the book.

✔ **On Compaq iPAQ Pocket PCs, use the Navigator button on the front of the Pocket PC to move through the book:** Pressing on the right side or the lower side of the button moves you forward, while pressing on the left side or the top side of the button moves you back.

> ✔ **On Casio Cassiopeia Pocket PCs, use the rocker switch on the left side of the Pocket PC the same way as you would use the HP Jornada rocker switch:** You can also use the Navigator button on the front of the Pocket PC the same way you use the Navigator button on the front of a Compaq iPAQ. You can even switch off between the two if your finger gets tired of paging through the book.

One thing that's very different about reading e-books on your Pocket PC compared to reading a text document on your desktop PC is that e-books always jump an entire page at a time. You don't see the line-by-line scrolling that's common when you're viewing text documents.

Adding notes and such

Have you ever found yourself writing notes on one of those sticky notepads and then placing the note into a book you're reading? Eventually, reading the book without knocking the notes out of place becomes almost impossible. And even if the notes stay where they belong, remembering where you made which note can be daunting.

When you're reading an e-book, though, adding your own notes to the text is really easy, as is going back later to reference to those notes. To do so, follow these steps:

1. **Highlight the word or phrase you wish to annotate.**

2. **Choose Add Note from the pop-up menu that appears as soon as you finish your highlighting.**

3. **Type in your note, as shown in Figure 2-6, and then tap Done to complete your note.**

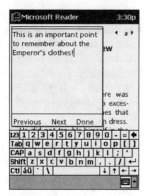

Figure 2-6: Add your own notes to e-books to help you find important points later.

After you add notes to the text, you can review your notes by using the annotation index. After you open the index, tap the note you'd like to see and the Reader opens not only the note, but also the page where you added the note.

Tap the keyboard icon to hide the onscreen keyboard when you're viewing existing notes. Doing so enables you to view the e-book page in addition to simply seeing the note itself.

You can also add highlighting, a bookmark, or a drawing to the text by selecting the proper choice from the pop-up menu that appears when you select text. If you want to quote the text exactly, you can copy the selected text.

Listening to Audio Books

At times, trying to read simply isn't convenient. Still, you may enjoy listening to something more intelligent than your average, self-absorbed, talk-radio host.

Your Pocket PC comes to the rescue by allowing you to listen to *audio books*. You can play these recorded books and other types of content, such as in-depth news reports, on your Pocket PC. Figure 2-7 shows one example of how this feature works. In this case, I'm listening to a 25-minute news broadcast that I downloaded from the Web in about a minute.

Figure 2-7: The Audible player enables Microsoft Reader to play back audio books that you download from the Web.

To use the Audible player you must first load it onto both your desktop PC and your Pocket PC. Some Pocket PCs include a version of the Audible player, but you can easily download the most recent version by visiting the Audible Web site at www.audible.com/. When you install the Audible player, it integrates with Microsoft Reader on your Pocket PC, and any audio book content you download appears in the Reader's library.

The download from Audible also includes the Audible Manager software for your desktop PC. This software makes easy work of downloading and managing content from the Audible Web site. Both the Audible Player and Audible Manager are free downloads. The Audible Web site includes some free content (along with several items that you must pay for).

Your Pocket PC can also play Windows Media Player compatible content. You don't play this type of material with the Microsoft Reader, but rather with the Windows Media Player built into your Pocket PC. You can find a huge variety of Windows Media Player content on the Web at sites such as Audiohighway (www.Audiohighway.com).

After you install the Audible Player and download some audio books to your Pocket PC, listening to an audio book is even easier than reading an e-book:

1. **Open Microsoft Reader, and then choose the audio book from your library.**

2. **Tap the play button (the single, right arrow in the toolbar).**

   The audio book begins playing. If you pause or stop the playback, the player remembers where you left off and resumes at the same point when you restart the playback later.

The headphones that come with your Pocket PC make audio books easier to understand, and avoid disturbing other people who don't want to hear your audio book.

The Audible Web site generally offers several different audio formats for download. Even though the site indicates that your Pocket PC may be able to use more than one of these formats, I've found that only format 1 — the most compressed and therefore lowest sound quality format — is actually compatible with Pocket PCs.

Chapter 3

That's Pocket PC Entertainment!

In This Chapter
▶ Playing music on your Pocket PC
▶ Playing games on your Pocket PC
▶ Using your Pocket PC as your digital camera's companion

*Y*ou probably didn't buy a Pocket PC just so you could work all the time. After all, even a busy person needs to relax sometimes. This chapter lets you in on some of the purely fun aspects of Pocket PC ownership.

Playing Music on Your Pocket PC

Your Pocket PC uses a special version of Windows Media Player to play music and other multimedia files. You can also use Windows Media Player on your desktop PC to create copies of music files for use on your Pocket PC.

Transferring music to your Pocket PC

Audio CDs are a great medium for distributing music. They're relatively small, fairly immune to casual damage, and they produce very high quality sound. But unless you have awfully big pockets, audio CDs aren't all that great as a portable music source. Not only are they too big, but they're also prone to skipping, even when played in really good portable CD players.

To copy music from an audio CD to your Pocket PC, follow these steps:

1. **Open Windows Media Player on your desktop PC.**

2. **Insert the audio CD into your CD drive.**

3. **Click the CD Audio button to display the tracks on the audio CD.**

   If you have an Internet connection, Windows Media Player attempts to obtain the track information from a music database located on the Internet.

4. **If you only want to copy certain tracks to your hard drive, make certain that only those tracks are checked before you click the Copy Music button.**

   Figure 3-1 shows how the Windows Media Player appears while it's copying the tracks.

Figure 3-1: Copy the music tracks to your desktop PC's hard drive first.

5. **Next click the Portable Device button.**

   Windows Media Player examines your Pocket PC to see how much space is available and then displays the music files in the currently open media library, as well as those on your Pocket PC.

6. **Select the tracks you want to copy to your Pocket PC, and then click the Copy Music button.**

Figure 3-2 shows how this process appears as files are being copied.

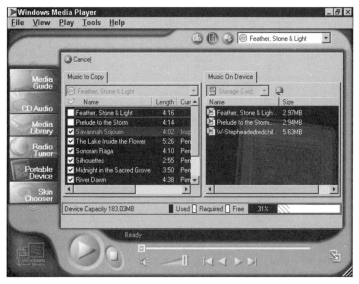

Figure 3-2: After the music is on your hard drive, you can copy it to your Pocket PC.

Creating a play list

After you have the music files on your Pocket PC, you can create a play list by selecting the music you would like to hear. If you have enough storage to store several different complete audio CDs on your Pocket PC, you may even want to create several different play lists.

To set up a play list, follow these steps:

1. **Click the Start button on your Pocket PC and choose Windows Media from the Start menu.**

2. **Tap Playlist on the menu bar, and then tap the + at the far left side of the toolbar that appears.**

3. **Select the songs you want to include, as shown in Figure 3-3, and then click OK.**

   If you want to rearrange the order of the tracks, use the up and down arrows in the toolbar to move tracks, and then tap OK.

Figure 3-3: Choose the songs you want in your play list.

Playing your music

After you set up your play list you can listen to the music. Figure 3-4 shows the Windows Media Player ready to begin playing.

To hear the recording in stereo, use the headphones that came with your Pocket PC. (If you're using the headphones that came with your Pocket PC, look for a small R on one earpiece and a small L on the other. That way you'll be certain that the right and left channels are playing in the correct ear.) You can also play back the music through a set of small battery powered amplified speakers like the ones often used with desktop PCs.

Music playback can be a major drain on your Pocket PC's battery; therefore, make sure that you start out with a fully charged battery, and turn off your Pocket PC's backlight. Some Pocket PCs, like the HP Jornada 540 series, enable you to turn off the entire display by pressing the button on the top of the Pocket PC.

Click here to play or pause

Click here to move back

Click here for track info

Click here to move forward

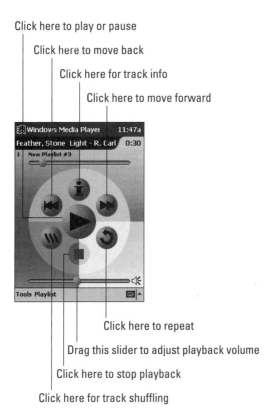

Click here to repeat

Drag this slider to adjust playback volume

Click here to stop playback

Click here for track shuffling

Figure 3-4: You're ready to enjoy the music you've stored on your Pocket PC.

Expanding your Pocket PC's musical capabilities

You may have noticed that my Pocket PC had quite a bit of room for storing music. One of the problems with using a Pocket PC as a portable music player is that you simply don't have much room for music files in the standard storage space that comes built into a Pocket PC. Fortunately, you can easily expand your Pocket PC's capacity by using a memory storage card. In my case, I added a 192 MB CF memory card from SanDisk to allow my Pocket PC to store several hours of music.

Different Pocket PCs have different types of expansion slots. Make certain that you know the exact type of slot your Pocket PC has before you buy an expansion card.

Finding music online

In addition to copying music from an audio CD, you can also find a good deal of music online that you can play on your Pocket PC. In some cases you can download free music tracks, but you also find artists who sell their own music online at a reasonable price.

Here are a few sites that allow you to download music:

- www.gigabeat.com
- www.mp3board.com
- www.mp3charts.com
- www.playdude.com
- www.soundhub.com
- www.windowsmedia.com

Playing Games on Your Pocket PC

You probably didn't buy a Pocket PC just so you could play games. You may even be one of those people who claim they never waste time playing games. Even so, aren't you at least curious to see just how good a Pocket PC game can be?

As you may guess, the fertile minds of game developers have created dozens of Pocket PC games. The games you can play on your Pocket PC run the gamut from deceptively simple to extremely complex. Some of the best of them are the ones that seem very simple but end up requiring a good deal of strategy to do well.

Most Pocket PC games are quite small, so downloading them from the Web is one of the best ways to get them. Many Pocket PC games are free, but you also find shareware games and commercial products at various sites. *Shareware programs* come in several varieties, but they all share one common thread — you get the chance to give them a try before you buy them. If you like the game, you send in a small amount of money to register your copy. Registration may add extra features, allow you to continue to use the game after the demo period expires, or simply ease your conscience knowing that you aren't stealing the results of someone else's work.

For freeware and shareware Pocket PC games you can download, one of the best places is the Tucows Web site at `pda.tucows.com/wince/`.

O Soli(taire) mio

Solitaire is probably the all-time favorite computer game, and it comes with your Pocket PC. Sure, lots of fun games have all sorts of fans, but Solitaire has probably burned up more computer time than virtually any other thing that people do with computers.

The following figure shows the Pocket PC version of Solitaire. To play Solitaire, do the following:

1. **Choose Start⇨Programs.**

2. **Tap the Games folder and choose Solitaire.**

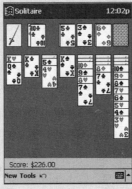

Your Pocket PC as Your Digital Camera Companion

If you have a digital camera in addition to your Pocket PC, you've probably thought about partnering the two devices. After all, your Pocket PC is a computer, and digital images are in their natural element on a computer. Why not use your Pocket PC to put those finishing touches on your digital images?

In order to work with digital images on your Pocket PC, you first have to move those images from your digital camera to your Pocket PC. This task is very simple in some cases and very difficult in others.

Sharing digital images on memory cards

The most straightforward method of sharing digital images between your digital camera and your Pocket PC is to use a memory storage card that is compatible with both units. If you have this option, you can typically just pop the memory card out of the camera, plug it into your Pocket PC, and you're ready to go — almost.

Your Pocket PC generally needs a bit of help finding files that are stored on a memory card if you haven't stored those files in a folder called My Documents. Digital cameras, of course, have no need for folders, so they simply store image files on the memory card without using any directory structure. Therefore, you may need to explicitly tell whatever software you're using on your Pocket PC to look on the storage card for image files, because they won't be stored in the Pocket PC's preferred location.

Connecting to your digital camera

As an alternative to sharing a memory card between your digital camera and your Pocket PC, you may want to transfer images another way — by connecting your Pocket PC and your digital camera. This option, however, may be even trickier to arrange than sharing a memory card.

Following are some possibilities for transferring images by connecting your Pocket PC and your digital camera:

- ✔ **Use the Image Expert CE software that is included with some Pocket PCs to transfer files directly from your digital camera:** If your Pocket PC didn't include the Image Expert CE software, you can download a trial version from www.sierraimaging.com/store/softwaretrials.html. Downloading the trial version allows you to determine whether your digital camera is supported.

- ✔ **Send images via infrared:** Some digital cameras also support sending images via infrared. This method may or may not work with your combination of digital camera and Pocket PC, but the two are more likely to be compatible if they're both from the same manufacturer.

- ✔ **Use the software that came with your digital camera to transfer from your digital camera to your desktop PC first:** Transferring image files to your desktop PC and then to your Pocket PC is the one foolproof method for moving your digital pictures. After you have the images on your desktop PC, use ActiveSync to send those files to your Pocket PC. Of course, this technique sort of defeats the whole idea of using your Pocket PC as your digital camera's companion, but it is a sure-fire approach.

Editing photos on your Pocket PC

Digital imaging is one place where the various Pocket PC manufacturers pretty much leave you on your own. You aren't going to find highly sophisticated photo editing software bundled with your Pocket PC. Fortunately, though, adding an inexpensive piece of software to your Pocket PC easily corrects the problem.

The tool I chose is Pocket Artist from Conduits Technologies. You can download a trial version from www.conduits.com/ce/artist/. Figure 3-5 shows an example of the items that are available on the Pocket Artist Menu⇨Tools menu.

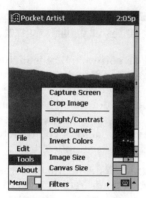

Figure 3-5: Pocket Artist gives you all the basic image editing tools you may want to use to fix up your digital photos.

When you take photos with your digital camera, you're likely to find that some adjustment of the brightness, contrast, or colors really improves the images. As Figure 3-5 shows, Pocket Artist gives you easy access to these adjustments.

If you want to go beyond basic adjustments and get creative, Pocket Artist provides tools to help there, too. For example, Figure 3-6 shows the list of tools that appear when you tap the paintbrush icon on the toolbar.

Figure 3-6: Pocket Artist also goes well beyond the basics with tools for artistic manipulation.

Part II
The Part of Tens

The 5th Wave   By Rich Tennant

"Yes I did have a date with Susan tonight, but she just downloaded 'How to Win Friends and Influence People' to her Pocket PC, so she stayed home to read it."

In this part . . .

This part has two fun chapters. The first one tells you a bunch of things that are good to tuck under your Pocket PC thinking cap. The second details all of the very cool applications included in the CD at the back of this book. Hurry, turn the page — I can't stand the excitement!

Chapter 4

Ten Good Things to Know about Pocket PCs

In This Chapter

▶ Understanding what you can and can't do with a Pocket PC

▶ Switching information from a Palm device to a Pocket PC

▶ Attaching a modem to your Pocket PC

▶ Increasing memory on your Pocket PC

▶ Networking with your Pocket PC

▶ Keeping your Pocket PC batteries charged

*T*he more you use your Pocket PC, the more you'll be amazed at what it can do. On the other hand, you may also be surprised at some of the things that Pocket PCs can't do — at least not yet. This chapter takes you through some of the features that you need to be aware of as a Pocket PC owner.

Recognizing What Will and Won't Work with Your Pocket PC

Before you go out and spend your money on Pocket PC accessories, you really need to know what will and what won't work with your Pocket PC. I can't think of much worse than getting all excited about some great gadget, buying it, and then finding out it doesn't work. Here are some guidelines to help you avoid this disappointment:

✔ **Not all Pocket PCs have the same type and size of expansion slot:** The most common one is the CF slot, but MMC expansion slots and PC Card expansion slots are also available.

✔ **Some Pocket PC CF slots are Type 1 slots:** If you're thinking about a CF slot device, remember that some CF devices require the thicker Type 2 slot and won't fit Pocket PCs with Type 1 slots. You can use Type 1 CF devices in Type 2 CF slots, but not the other way around. You can use CF devices in PC Card slots by obtaining an inexpensive adapter; however, you can't make PC Card devices fit a CF slot.

✔ **Pocket PCs generally have a serial connection, but you may need to buy a special cable from your Pocket PC's manufacturer to connect to standard serial devices:** External modems fall into this category.

✔ **Some serial devices won't work with a Pocket PC (even if you have the correct cable):** Anything that needs special driver software will only work if it includes a driver specifically designed for the Pocket PC. Drivers intended for the version of Windows on your desktop PC won't work on your Pocket PC.

✔ **Some devices are designed to work with specific Pocket PC processors:** If the package lists SH3, MIPS, or Arm processors, check to see that the processor in your Pocket PC is one that is supported.

One sure way to find Pocket PC accessories that will work with your Pocket PC is to visit your Pocket PC manufacturer's Web site. You may even find that the manufacturer offers special deals for owners of their brand of Pocket PC.

You can expand all Pocket PCs, but the brand and model you own may limit your options. The following list shows the type of expansion available on some common Pocket PC models:

✔ **Most Casio Pocket PCs include a CF Type 2 expansion slot:** These models can use any CF expansion device compatible with Pocket PCs.

✔ **Some Casio models — notably the EM-500 — include an MMC expansion slot:** This smaller-size slot generally limits any expansion possibilities to an MMC memory card.

✔ **HP Pocket PCs include a CF Type 1 expansion slot:**
Because the Type 1 slot is thinner than the Type 2 slot,
HP Pocket PCs can't use a few CF expansion devices that
require Type 2 slots.

✔ **Compaq iPAQ Pocket PCs don't include any expansion
slots:** If you want to add on to your Compaq iPAQ Pocket
PC, you have to buy an expansion sleeve. These sleeves
are available in both CF Type 2 and PC Card models.
Because the PC Card model can also accommodate CF
devices by using an inexpensive adapter, the PC Card
sleeve is a far better choice.

Moving Info from a Palm Device into Your Pocket PC

Moving from a Palm device to a Pocket PC is really a huge step
up. Your Pocket PC has far more power, lots more memory,
and many more capabilities than a Palm device. But if you've
been using your Palm device for some time, you probably
have quite a bit of information stored in it and aren't looking
forward to re-entering all of that information into your new
Pocket PC. Frankly, I don't blame you. Who wants to work that
hard when there's an easier way?

Your Palm device and your Pocket PC can share information,
and it doesn't take a rocket scientist to make it work. What it
does take is some software that understands how to do the
job. You can move data from your Palm device to your Pocket
PC in several ways, but the basic process goes like this:

1. **Use the Palm Desktop software to connect your Palm
   device to your desktop PC.**

2. **Add in a piece of software that understands how to
   translate information between the Palm device and
   Outlook.**

3. **Send the information to Outlook on your desktop PC
   from the Palm device.**

4. **Connect your Pocket PC to your desktop PC by using
   ActiveSync.**

5. **Synchronize your Pocket PC and your desktop PC.**

Connecting your Palm device with your desktop PC

Your Palm device comes with software called Palm Desktop. If you don't have the latest version, you may want to visit www.palm.com/support/downloads to make certain you have a copy that includes any recent updates, but this step probably won't be necessary — especially since you aren't likely to keep using your Palm device after you start using a Pocket PC.

Before you move on to the next step, be sure that the Palm Desktop software is installed on your desktop PC and that the Palm device is turned on and connected to your desktop PC through whatever cradle or synchronization cable came with it.

Adding software to connect the Palm device to Outlook

Next you have to add some software to your desktop PC that understands how to translate between the Palm device files and Outlook. Several choices are available, and you may already have one of them on the CD-ROM that came with your Palm device:

- ✔ **Pocket Mirror:** This software is supplied with many Palm devices, so it's a good solution if you have it. You can also check out the Chapura Web site at www.chapura.com for updates.

- ✔ **CompanionLink:** Another excellent option, I show this one in my examples. One big advantage that Companion-Link has over almost any other of the data conversion programs is that this same software understands both the Palm device and the Pocket PC. You can find CompanionLink at www.companionlink.com/clx.htm.

- ✔ **Desktop To Go:** Desktop To Go provides a bit more control over the conversion process — which may be very helpful if you need to move data to different fields as you transfer it. Unfortunately, Desktop To Go only works with Palm devices, so you may not have much use for the program after you move from the Palm device to your new Pocket PC. You'll find Desktop To Go at www.dataviz.com/products/desktoptogo/index.html.

You can download 15-day trial versions of both CompanionLink and Desktop To Go from the Web. In most cases you'll probably only be transferring data from your Palm device to your Pocket PC once, so the trial version should be more than adequate to fill your needs.

Whichever conversion software you choose, download and install it before you continue.

Here's an example of setting up CompanionLink to handle the conversion from the Palm device to Outlook:

1. **Run the CompanionLink setup program to install CompanionLink on your desktop PC.**

   Run CompanionLink Setup by choosing the program from your Start menu or by opening the icon on your desktop.

2. **Choose the type of device, as shown in Figure 4-1.**

   You're given a number of options — be sure that you select the correct one. Click Next after you make your selection.

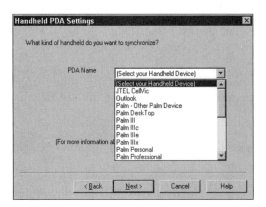

Figure 4-1: Choose your Palm device from the list.

3. Select Outlook 2000 in the PIM Name box, as shown in Figure 4-2.

You can also use CompanionLink to synchronize with other applications, but you must use Outlook while you're transferring the data from the Palm device to your Pocket PC.

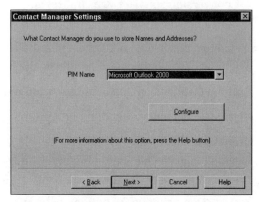

Figure 4-2: Choose Outlook 2000 as the Contact Manager.

4. Click Configure so you can adjust the transfer settings.

5. Select the Add Handheld Info to the PC option, as shown in Figure 4-3, and then click OK.

Doing so makes the synchronization go a bit faster, and ensures that you don't encounter errors as a result of sending too much Outlook data to the Palm device.

6. Click Next to display the message shown in Figure 4-4, and then click Finish to complete the setup.

Notice in the figure that not all information is automatically sent from your Palm device to Outlook on your desktop PC. If you have additional information that you want to transfer, use the options in the dialog box shown in Figure 4-3 to set this up.

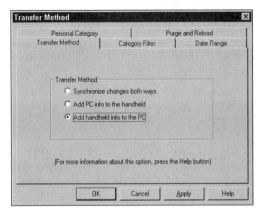

Figure 4-3: Make sure that data only goes from the Palm device to your desktop PC.

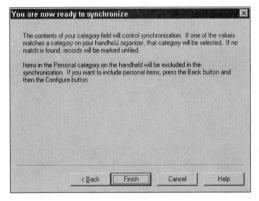

Figure 4-4: You're now ready to begin sending info to Outlook.

Sending data from the Palm device to Outlook

After you set up CompanionLink or some other conversion software properly, you can send the data from your Palm device to Outlook on your desktop PC. Here's how to send data by using CompanionLink:

1. **Start CompanionLink by choosing the CompanionLink Synchronize program from your Start menu or by opening the icon on your desktop.**

   If you don't want to include all of the information from your Palm device, click the Category Manager button and choose the categories you do want to send.

2. **Click the Synchronize button and wait while the information transfers to Outlook.**

3. **Check your desktop PC to make certain that all of the information was correctly transferred into Outlook.**

Moving the data to your Pocket PC

Once you transfer the information from your Palm device to Outlook, the rest of the process is really easy:

1. **Turn off your Palm device or remove it from the cradle to prevent interference with your Pocket PC.**

2. **Place your Pocket PC into its own synchronization cradle and wait as ActiveSync automatically adds the new information that was on the Palm device.**

3. **Find some unsuspecting soul and give him your old Palm device — you aren't going to have much use for it anymore!**

If some information was transferred from your Palm device to Outlook, but not from Outlook to your Pocket PC, click the Options button in ActiveSync and make certain that you selected all of the correct categories.

Adding Memory

Without any question, my favorite Pocket PC accessory is additional storage. Because Pocket PCs store everything in memory, you can quickly use up the available memory when you get carried away with adding new programs, e-books, music, or whatever to your Pocket PC. In fact, that's one of the main hazards of the Pocket PC's versatility — users tend to dream up all sorts of great things they can do with them.

 As with all Pocket PC expansion options, make sure that you know what type of memory card will fit your Pocket PC before you buy.

Adding a Modem

Modems connect your Pocket PC to the Internet so you can use e-mail and browse your favorite Web sites. Two types of modems are available for the Pocket PC — wired and wireless. Wireless modems may be cool and sexy, but they're also slow and expensive compared to wired modems. If you just can't live without a wireless modem, you'll probably end up getting a wired modem, too, just so you can get stuff done faster.

Wired modems

Wired modems for the Pocket PC can be external ones that connect through the serial connector, or they can be internal ones that pop into the CF expansion slot. Each has its advantages:

- ✔ **CF modems slip right into your Pocket PC so you don't have to use the serial connector:** Not only do you get a smaller package, but you can also use the CF modem while your Pocket PC is connected to an external keyboard.

- ✔ **External modems either include a cable that plugs into your Pocket PC's serial connector or they connect directly to a serial cable that came with your Pocket PC:** If you get an external modem that plugs into the serial connector, it will likely be one that you buy directly from the Pocket PC's manufacturer. If the modem uses your Pocket PC's serial cable, you may have to buy the cable separately.

> ✔ If you want to use a memory card or other device that fits into the expansion slot, you won't be able to use it at the same time as a CF modem.

If you have a serial cable for your Pocket PC, you can use almost any external modem — you don't need a special Pocket PC-compatible external modem.

Wireless modems

Wireless modems enable your Pocket PC to connect anywhere — sort of. You can connect anywhere as long as that "anywhere" is within the coverage area of your wireless service provider and you can get a strong enough signal.

Connecting to Your Network

Your Pocket PC normally connects to your desktop PC by using a USB connection, or in some cases by using a standard serial connection. You may find that these types of connections simply aren't convenient in your case. If so, you can also connect by using an Ethernet adapter in your Pocket PC to make a network connection. In fact, you can use ActiveSync to synchronize your Pocket PC over your network.

If all you need to do is to connect your Pocket PC and your desktop PC, you need a *crossover* cable or a crossover coupling between the two. If you want to use a standard network cable, you need to connect your Pocket PC to the network hub or switch rather than directly to your desktop PC. A network connection will probably be faster than either a USB or standard serial connection when you're transferring files. Speed probably won't make much difference, however, unless you've added a very large capacity memory card to your Pocket PC and are moving a huge amount of data.

Powering Your Way to Freedom

The next accessory isn't as cool or neat as some of the others in this chapter, but it's still something no Pocket PC user should be without. Pocket PCs all run on batteries, and they're automatically recharged whenever your Pocket PC is placed into the synchronization cradle. And because your Pocket PC uses very aggressive power management, in normal use a Pocket PC runs a long time — anywhere from five to ten hours — on a single charge.

Okay, so your Pocket PC runs a long time on a charge. That doesn't mean it can run forever. Eventually you have to recharge the batteries or your Pocket PC will die. And since you can't just pop in a fresh set of batteries from the drugstore, that means you have to bring your Pocket PC home and place it into the synchronization cradle for refueling.

So what does this have to do with a great Pocket PC accessory? Simple — you need a second power adapter for your Pocket PC so you can charge up the batteries no matter where you are. I recommend one that plugs into your car's cigarette lighter so you can use your Pocket PC while you're traveling. You may also want to buy a second AC adapter so you don't have to unplug the one on your desk.

The best source of power adapters for your Pocket PC is your Pocket PC's manufacturer. But if you're going to be traveling in foreign countries, then also go to the iGo Web site (www.igo.com) to pick up the necessary plug adapters and transformers so you can use different voltages without harming your Pocket PC.

Chapter 5

Slightly More than Ten Pocket PC Applications

In This Chapter

▶ Pocket PC utility applications

▶ Pocket PC game applications

*S*oftware developers everywhere are creating applications that you can add to your Pocket PC. These applications include utilities to make your life easier and games to make your life more fun. As an added bonus, the CD in the back of this book contains several applications that you can download to your Pocket PC; this chapter describes each of them.

Golfwits by SiscoSoft

Golfwits — a computer application that runs on Windows-powered Laptop, Desktop, and Pocket PCs — includes a user-friendly interface that enables golfers to take their game to a new level of performance and enjoyment. Golfwits' exclusive MIMO (Minimum Input, Maximum Output) technology allows you to do the following:

- ✔ **Record the ball position, distance, shot shape, and club you use for every shot with just three taps on the screen.**

- ✔ **Track and save rounds for up to four players per round:** You can then view, print, and e-mail this information.

- ✔ **Customize your stats to track any aspect of your game virtually.**

- ✔ **E-mail a Viewer file of your round for others to see.**

Pocket Golfwits enables you to record your play (and the play of up to three other golfers) on a detailed map of each hole of your course; Golfwits automatically posts your score and tracks your statistics. Designed for on-course use with a new Pocket PC, Pocket Golfwits is your digital "yardage book." Each round's details are saved for future review and game improvement.

Using Pocket Golfwits on a Pocket PC while playing your round is the ultimate way to

✔ **Score your round.**

✔ **Find distances to trouble.**

✔ **Place your shots on the course map while you play.**

✔ **View statistics mid-round.**

Used in conjunction with SiscoSoft's interactive digital course maps, Golfwits automatically tracks visual patterns of play and a host of comprehensive statistics for each of your golf rounds. You can use this information to customize a playing strategy that helps you improve play on each course that you build a history for.

At home you can copy your round to your desktop computer, and, if you have Golfwits PC, you can review your round and print out a scorecard or trophy sheet. Golfwits prints great in color and works on grayscale printers as well.

Mapwits is a versatile software tool that creates digital, inter-active Golfwits course maps. You can make your own GWC maps of your favorite course or edit any GWC map to add your own features. If the Golfwits map for your course is not available yet, you can produce your own! Download Mapwits for Windows 95/98/NT, a straightforward map-making tool that enables you to create full-featured Golfwits maps.

Developer One Agenda Today v3.01

Developer One Agenda Today delivers an innovative way to quickly and efficiently view and manage your busy schedule right from your Pocket PC's today page. In addition to enhancing your Pocket PC's today page, Agenda Today includes a powerful and easy-to-use, 7-day, schedule-manager application that gives you an at-a-glance view of all of the details for an entire week of your appointments and tasks. (The CD in the back of this book provides a full-featured, 14-day trial.)

Agenda Today works as the perfect companion to the built-in Pocket Outlook applications on your Pocket PC, giving you a highly optimized view of your schedule, even displaying birthdays and anniversaries from your contacts list. You can easily configure Agenda Today to launch directly from your tasks and appointments applications, giving you instant access to your 7-day agenda view from anywhere on your Pocket PC.

You can tailor Agenda Today to meet your exact schedule management preferences. Agenda Today includes innovative features such as drag-and-drop appointment and task creation and daily time status indicators for a quick reference of your daily schedule. You're in complete control of the items shown in your agenda, including color customization, category icon display, multiple categories filtering, and much more.

Developer One ScreenSnap v5.1

With Developer One ScreenSnap, you can instantly capture and organize Pocket PC screen images in a file, and then transfer them to your host PC at any time. ScreenSnap also allows you to do the following:

- ✔ **Record your application settings — such as network and communications settings — and options for future reference.**
- ✔ **Create application documentation and user's guides.**

✓ **Put together graphical presentations on your desktop:**
You can download the image files to your Pocket PC, and
browse them by using the full-screen, button-activated
view mode.

✓ **Assist with presentations by acting as an electronic
note-card viewer:** You can create images on your desktop PC that contain your reference material, download
them to your Pocket PC, and view them one-handed with
the buttons on your Pocket PC.

Tipster by Ilium Software

With one touch, Tipster gives you your tip or tax amount both
by itself and added to your original amount. One more touch
divides the total by any number you select. Adjust the tip or
tax percentage with just one more touch — and never re-enter
your original amount. Tipster can even calculate your before-
tax tip amount. To calculate tips or sales tax, do this:

1. **Configure the default percentages you want to use
   for tips and tax by choosing Tools⇨Options.**

2. **Enter the amount of your bill by tapping it in on the
   on-screen keypad.**

3. **Tap one of the buttons on the right — Tax, Tip, Big
   Tip, or Small Tip — to enter the proper percentage
   into the calculation.**

   Tipster automatically calculates the tip or tax amount,
   and the total of the bill with tip or tax. If you want to
   give a slightly larger — or slightly smaller — tip, you
   can adjust the percentage up or down by tapping the
   up-down control next to the percentage.

   If you want to calculate the amount of your tip before
   tax, check the Calculate Tip Before Tax option, enter
   your bill (including tax), and select one of the Tip buttons. Tipster automatically deducts the tax (by using
   the default tax percent you set) before calculating the
   tip amount.

4. **When splitting the bill with several people, enter the
   number of people present into the box below the
   total.**

Tipster divides the total by that number to calculate each person's share of the bill.

For more information about Ilium Software and its other Pocket PC applications, visit www.iliumsoft.com or call 888-632-5388.

eWallet by Ilium Software

eWallet is an electronic wallet for your most important personal information. Use eWallet to store your credit cards, calling cards, bank account numbers, passwords, PIN numbers, and more. You can create as many different wallets as you need, and you can organize your information in the way that best fits your needs and style. Each wallet can contain as many *categories* as you want. Categories are a way to organize your *cards*, which contain your actual information. You must have one password per wallet, but you can set your password on or off per category. If a category is password-protected, you must enter the wallet's password before you can see the information on any of the cards in that category. Card information is only encrypted for those cards stored in password-protected categories.

Give your cards names with meaning so that you can locate and reference them easily. All the information on each card is optional, so enter only the information you need. Use the Other Information field (on cards that have it) to enter additional information you want to see on your card, for example, instructions for using a calling card or additional phone numbers. Use the Notes Pane for lengthier notes and information you'd like to associate with a card. You can change any of the information in any of the cards at any time by using the Properties tool, or change the name of any cards by using the Rename menu pick.

In addition to using cards that allow you to store all sorts of general information, eWallet also has specific cards for the following tasks:

- ✔ **Banking:** Account numbers for your financial accounts and credit card numbers, for example

- ✔ **Health and safety information:** Fire, ambulance, police, and other emergency telephone numbers, for example

✔ **Identification and contact:** Telephone calling cards, with access numbers and PIN numbers, for example

✔ **Personal information:** Auto, life, home, and other insurance policies, including the number to call for claims, for example

✔ **Travel information:** Your passport information, for example

More information about eWallet is available on the Internet at www.iliumsoft.com/wallet.htm or by calling 888-632-5388.

ZIOGolf

If you have your Pocket PC, you're one tap away from the excitement of a true golf game. ZIOGolf, a real-time 3D golf game, provides a perfect getaway whether you're at the office, in an airline terminal, or lounging at home. (ZIO Interactive, Inc., also provides various real golf courses separately.)

Bubblets

Read no further if you have deadlines to meet. Bubblets is a totally addictive Pocket PC puzzle game. The object of the game is simple: The more bubbles you burst at once, the more points you receive. Tap a group of similar bubbles to select the group and then tap them again in order to burst them from the board. Plan your strategy wisely to win big points. Plan poorly and you're stuck with nothing!

Hearts

Hearts is an infrared game that you can play with another person who also has Hearts on a Pocket PC and is using the infrared port.

The object of Hearts is to have the lowest score at the end of the game. Players win cards, which are tallied at the end of each hand. Each heart counts as one point, and the queen of spades is worth 13 points. However, a player who *shoots the moon* — wins all of the hearts and the queen of spades in a single hand — receives no points for that hand, but each opponent gets 26 points. The game is over when one player's score reaches 100 or when 10 hands have been played, whichever comes first.

Hearts is one of the games in the Entertainment Pack for the Pocket PC. For more information, please go to www.pocketpc.com.

Windows Media Player

Windows Media Player offers the best player experience on the Handheld PC for the download, personalization, and playback of high-quality Windows Media audio and the popular MP3 format. For more information on Windows Media Player, refer to Chapter 3, "That's Pocket PC Entertainment!"

PowerToys

If you're a Pocket PC power-user, go ahead and try these out. Great care has been taken to ensure that PowerToys operate as they should. But please note that Microsoft is making these tools available to you on the CD "as is"; Microsoft doesn't support them, so Microsoft Technical Support is unable to answer questions about PowerToys.

Microsoft Power Contacts for Pocket PCs

This PowerToy adds the following options to the Contacts pop-up menu:

- ✔ **Create Appointment:** Creates an appointment with the contact as the attendee and the subject.

- ✔ **Create Task:** Creates a task with the contact as the subject.

- ✔ **Open Web Page:** Opens the Web page associated with the contact.

Microsoft Today Screen Image Tool for Pocket PCs

Always wanted to customize your Today Screen? Well now you can! This PowerToy allows you to add your favorite picture to the Today screen.

Windows Media Skin Chooser for Pocket PCs

By using the Windows Media Skin Chooser, you can change the Windows Media Player's interface to match your personality or your music. *Skins* are the custom interface created for the Windows Media Player. A skin is a collection of bitmap files (files with the .bmp extension) and a text file (in this case, a file with a .skn extension). You can use information stored in the .skn file to organize the images, giving you complete control over what buttons you want, how they look, and where they're located onscreen. For more skin options go to www.microsoft.com/windows/windowsmedia/en/software/players/Skins.asp.

ActiveSync Extras

You can find lots of great add-ons for your Pocket PC on the ActiveSync 3.1 CD included with your Pocket PC, but in case you don't have that handy, here are a couple of must-haves.

Microsoft Pocket Streets

Pocket Streets — included in Microsoft Streets and Trips 2001, AutoRoute 2001 (European maps), and Microsoft MapPoint 2001 business-mapping software — delivers thousands of miles of street-map information to your Pocket PC. Creating custom maps of cities, towns, or villages you're traveling to is now easier than ever. With Pocket Streets you can:

✔ **Create your own personal street-level detail maps:** Just select the map area you want to copy from Streets & Trips 2001 and download it to your Pocket PC.

> ✔ Quickly pinpoint addresses, towns, intersections, hotels, restaurants, ATM machines, and over 600,000 other points of interest.
>
> ✔ Customize your maps by importing your favorite places and points of interest with Pushpins.

Follow these simple steps to try Pocket Streets and free sample maps right now:

1. **Make sure that ActiveSync 3.1 is installed on your desktop PC, and that your Pocket PC is connected to your desktop by using a serial cable or docking cradle.**

   If you don't already have Pocket Streets on your Pocket PC, download and install it now. *Note:* If you have a previous version of Pocket Streets installed, you must uninstall it before installing Version 2001. You can uninstall it from your device by using Remove Programs in Settings.

2. **Click on the name of the city map you want to download.**

   You can download some cities for free from `www.microsoft.com/pocketpc/downloads/streets.asp`

3. **Choose Save to disk when prompted to Open or Save the file.**

4. **Save the maps to the hard drive on your Windows 95/98/NT operating system.**

5. **Use ActiveSync to transfer maps to your Pocket PC.**

   For easiest use, save your maps in the My Documents directory.

Microsoft Transcriber

Some Pocket PC-based applications have small cramped keyboards, or no keyboard at all. Transcriber frees you from the constraints imposed by these applications and unleashes their power. Microsoft Transcriber is an award-winning application that uses proprietary Transcriber technology to bring unprecedented recognition accuracy and ease of use to your

Pocket PC. Transcriber lets you take down a phone number, notes, and more, just as easily and naturally as writing on a piece of paper. Transcriber recognizes all handwriting whether cursive, print, or a combination of both.

Transcriber employs advanced fuzzy logic and neural net techniques that allow it to recognize your handwriting with unparalleled accuracy and speed. Think your handwriting is too messy for Transcriber to make sense of? Chances are, you'll be pleasantly surprised. In addition to recognizing letters, numbers, and words, Transcriber recognizes common symbols and various control "gestures."

BSQUARE

BSQUARE is innovating tomorrow's devices through software solutions for the development of intelligent computing devices. Specializing in the Microsoft Windows family of operating systems, BSQUARE supplies software products and services for the development and use of PC companions, set-top boxes, Web pads, Internet appliances, industrial automation devices, Windows-based terminals, and other mobile and wireless intelligent devices. For more information, visit BSQUARE at www.bsquare.com.

BSQUARE bUseful Utilities Pak

bUseful 2.0 Utilities Pak (a 30-day evaluation is included on the CD in the back of this book) is designed to provide you with a suite of ten applications to avoid data loss disasters, and make your device faster and easier to use. The bUseful Utilities Pak includes ten applications:

- **bUseful Backup Plus:** Avoid potential data loss by backing up all data or portions of data on a device in under a minute.

- **bUseful Analyzer:** Use this industry standard to analyze and benchmark every portion of a PC Companion system and to compare multiple units.

- **bUseful Zip:** Enable industry-standard file compression for easy storage on PC Companions.

✔ **bUseful Script:** Automate routine tasks for a Pocket PC, such as logging on to an ISP address. Now includes support for JScript and VBscript for full macro capabilities.

✔ **bUseful Scheduler:** Schedule your automatic device tasks.

✔ **bUseful Launch:** Save time by creating a customized start menu for the fast launching of items you use the most: folders, programs, files, Web sites, and so on.

✔ **bUseful Notepad:** Edit and create text files quickly and easily.

✔ **bUseful FindSpace:** Free up memory to improve device performance.

✔ **bTask:** Navigate applications, close applications, and view device information, including storage and battery status.

✔ **bFind:** Never lose track of information again with this global search utility that searches for files, file contents, databases, contacts, and more.

BSQUARE bFax 5.0

bFax Pro 5.0 (a 30-day evaluation is included on the CD in the back of this book) is a powerful productivity tool that allows you to send and receive faxes directly via Internet faxing support, a modem and phone line, or a mobile phone. With bFax, you can do the following:

✔ **Edit and sign documents on the device with Inking:** You can also Annotate documents with a handwritten note or adjust your documents' fonts and margins.

✔ **Save on phone charges with offline rendering:** You can also enjoy peace of mind when sending to international numbers with bFax Pro's support for foreign number conventions.

✔ **Send multiple documents to multiple recipients:** You can send faxes to recipients in your Contacts database by simply tapping on the screen.

✔ **Send and receive faxes by using the Internet and BSQUARE's Internet Faxing Service Partners.**

> ✔ **Save time and money by previewing your fax before sending it by using bPrint, which is included:** bFax also lets you create and manage recurring faxes. You can send Pocket Word, text, bitmap, tiff, Pocket Excel, or any other document from any application that supports printing.

BSQUARE Messenger 1.1

BSQUARE Messenger turns Pocket PCs into an instant communications tool. Communicate real-time with Windows-powered device users and the more than 62 million Hotmail users around the world. Use the open, free, and widely accessible Hotmail Web-based system to transmit messages. BSQUARE Messenger is a smart alternative to proprietary technology that restricts users to communicate strictly within fee-based systems. Corporations use Messenger for intra-company communications via wireless LAN; sales representatives and other mobile professionals communicate back to company headquarters.

BSQUARE Messenger allows you to do the following:

> ✔ **Instantly view which friends and colleagues are on- or offline.**

> ✔ **Quickly send messages with a fast double-tap on the contact.**

> ✔ **Wirelessly communicate with friends and family while away from home or office.**

Index

• A •

accessories, 56
ActiveSync, 57, 62, 64
  add-ons, 74–75
ActiveSync CD-ROM, 33
adding
  memory, 63
  modems, 63–64
Add Note command, 39
Agenda Today, 69
analog phone lines, 9
applications, 67–78
Arm processors, 56
Audible Manager, 41
Audible player, 41
Audible Web site, 41, 42
audio books, 40–42
audio CDs, 43–45
audio formats, 42
Audiohighway Web site, 41

• B •

backlit screen, 32
bFind, 77
bookmarks, 40
browsing Web sites, 22
BSQUARE, 76–77
BSQUARE bFax, 77–78
BSQUARE bUseful Utilities Pak, 76–77
BSQUARE Messenger, 78
BSQUARE Web site, 76
bTask, 77
Bubblets, 72
bUseful Analyzer, 76
bUseful Backup Plus, 76
bUseful FindSpace, 77
bUseful Launch, 77
bUseful Notepad, 77
bUseful Scheduler, 77
bUseful Script, 77
bUseful Zip, 76

• C •

Casio Pocket PCs, 39, 56
CDPD (Cellular Digital Packet Data)
  service, 9
cell phones
  dial tone, 17
  digital phone cards, 8
cell service provider access service
  number, 16
CF digital phone cards, 10
CF modems, 63–64
CF slots, 8, 56
  See also Type 1 or 2 CF slots
Chapura Web site, 58
Compact Flash (CF) wired modems, 10
CompanionLink, 58–59
CompanionLink setup program, 59
CompanionLink Synchronize, 62
CompanionLink Web site, 58
Compaq iPAQ Pocket PCs, 8
  expansion slots, 57
  navigating e-books, 38
  wireless modems, 10
Conduits Technologies Web site, 51
connecting
  to digital cameras, 50–51
  to Internet *See* Internet connections
  to networks, 64
Connections folder, 15, 22
Connect to screen, 14–16
copying e-books to Pocket PCs, 33
crossover cable, 64
crossover coupling, 64

• D •

Dataviz Web site, 58
deleting
  e-books, 35
  e-mail, 28
  files, 36
desktop PCs, 58

Desktop To Go, 58–59
Developer One Agenda Today, 69
Developer One ScreenSnap, 69–70
digital cameras, 50–51
digital images
  editing, 51–52
  infrared transfer of, 51
  sharing on memory cards, 50
digital phone cards, 8, 16–17
digital phone lines, 9
DNS addresses, 14
downloading e-books, 33–34
drawings, 40
drives, 56

● *E* ●

E-Book Connection Web site, 32, 34
eBook Directory Web site, 34
e-books, 31
  adding notes, 39–40
  bookmarks, 40
  compressed format, 32
  deleting, 35
  downloading, 33–34
  drawings, 40
  First Page, 37
  highlighting, 40
  library, 36
  managing, 35
  memory storage, 35
  Microsoft Reader, 31–32, 34
  navigating, 37–39
  reading, 36–37
  read only file attribute, 34
  reviewing notes, 40
editing digital images, 51–52
e-mail, 23–30
  deleting, 28
  including original message in, 27–28
  mail servers, 23
  message creation, 29
  options, 27–28
  saving copy of, 28
  sending and receiving, 28–30
  sending and receiving automatically,
    25
  setting up account, 23–27
  urgent messages, 27
Encarta Pocket Dictionary file, 36
Ethernet adapter, 64
eWallet, 71–72

expansion slots, 48, 56–57
external modems, 63

● *F* ●

File Explorer, 36
files, deleting or moving, 36

● *G* ●

games, 48–49
General tab, 19–20
Gigabeat Web site, 48
Golfwits, 67–68
Golfwits PC, 68

● *H* ●

hardware, 7–8
  CF digital phone cards, 10
  CF slot, 8
  Compact Flash (CF) wired modems, 10
  digital phone cards, 8
  Minstrel wireless modems, 11
  options, 10–11
  PC Card slots, 8
  wired modems, 8
  wireless modems, 10
headphones, 42, 46
Hearts, 72
highlighting e-books, 40
home pages, 23
HP Jornada 540 series Pocket PCs, 11
  CF Type 1 expansion slots, 57
  navigating e-books, 38
  turning off display, 46

● *I* ●

IDG Books Worldwide, Inc. Web site, 22
iGo Web site, 65
Image Expert CE, 51
incoming mail servers, 25
infrared transfer of digital images, 51
Internet connections, 7
  automatically establishing, 21
  hardware options, 10–11
  listing, 12
  naming, 13
  opening, 22

service availability, 9
setting up, 11–17
type, 21, 25
ISPs (Internet Service Providers), 14–15

• *L* •

links, 22–23

• *M* •

mail servers, 23–25
Make New Connection screen, 13
Mapwits, 68
memory
  adding, 63
  storage for e-books, 35
memory cards, 47
  CF modems, 64
  sharing digital images, 50
Microsoft Pocket Streets, 74–75
Microsoft Power Contacts for
    Pocket PCs, 73
Microsoft Reader, 31–32, 36
  arrows for navigation, 38
  audio books, 42
Microsoft Reader-compatible files, 34
Microsoft Today Screen Image Tool for
    Pocket PCs, 74
Microsoft Transcriber, 75–76
Microsoft Web site, 74, 75
Minstrel wireless modems, 11
MIPS processors, 56
MMC expansion slots, 56
Modem Connections screen, 12–13
modems, 9, 63–64
moving
  data to Pocket PCs, 62
  files, 36
MP3 Board Web site, 48
MP3 Charts Web site, 48
music, 43
  battery drain, 46
  expanding Pocket PC capabilities,
      47–48
  finding online, 48
  playing, 46
  play list, 45–46
  stereo, 46
  transferring to Pocket PC, 43–45

• *N* •

navigating
  e-books, 37–39
  Web pages, 19
networks, connecting to, 64
Novatel Wireless Web site, 11

• *O* •

outgoing mail servers, 25
Outlook
  connecting Palm device, 58–60
  sending information from Palm
      device, 62

• *P* •

Palm Desktop, 58
Palm devices
  connecting to desktop PC, 58
  moving information from, 57–62
  sending data to Outlook, 62
  software, 58–60
Palm Web site, 58
passwords, saving, 16
PC Card Expansion Adapter sleeve, 8
PC Card slots, 8, 56
phone jacks, 9
Play Dude Web site, 48
playing music, 46
Pocket Artist, 51
Pocket Golfwits, 67–68
Pocket Internet Explorer, 17
  address bar, 22
  automatically opening Internet
      connection, 21
  connection options, 20–21
  general options, 19–20
  history list, 20
  navigating Web pages, 19
  screen, 18–19
  Web pages, 18, 20
Pocket Mirror, 58
Pocket PCs, 1
  Audible player, 41
  backlit screen, 32
  CF slot, 8
  copying e-books to, 33
  expanding, 48, 56–57

Pocket PCs *(cont.)*,
  hardware, 7–8
  headphones, 42, 46
  memory storage card, 47
  moving data to, 62
  setting up connection, 11–17
  size, 31
  turning off display, 46
  what will and will not work with, 55–56
  Windows Media Player, 41
Pocket PC StarterPak For Dummies CD,
  80
Pocket PC Web site, 73
Pocket Streets, 74–75
power adapters, 65
Power Toys, 73
programs, 67–78
proxy, 21
proxy server, 21

• *R* •

reading e-books, 36–37
recharging batteries, 65
removing temporary Web pages, 20

• *S* •

saving
  copy of e-mail, 28
  passwords, 16
ScreenSnap, 69–70
sending and receiving e-mail, 28–30
serial connections, 56
serial devices, 56
service availability, 9
Service Name screen, 23–24
Services⇨New Service command, 23
Settings dialog box, 12
setting up
  digital phone card connection, 16–17
  wired modem connection, 11–16
  wireless modem connection, 17
shareware programs, 49
sharing links, 22
SH3 processors, 56
Sierra Imaging Web site, 51
skins, 74
Solitaire, 49
Sound Hub Web site, 48
Start⇨Inbox command, 23

Start⇨Programs command, 15, 22,
  36, 49
Start⇨Settings command, 12

• *T* •

Tipster, 70–71
toggle, 22
Tools⇨Options command, 19, 70
Tools⇨Send Link via E-mail
  command, 22
Transcriber, 76
transferring music to your Pocket PC,
  43–45
Tucows Web site, 49
Type 1 CF slots, 8, 56–57
Type 2 CF slots, 8, 56

• *U* •

URL, 22

• *V* •

View⇨Address Bar command, 22

• *W* •

Web, 23
Web browsers, 17
Web browsing, 22
Web pages
  links, 23
  navigating, 19
  Pocket Internet Explorer, 18
  removing temporary, 20
  sending link to share, 22
  specific start-up, 20
Web sites, 22
Windows Media Player, 41, 44, 46, 73
Windows Media Skin Chooser for
  Pocket PCs, 74
Windows Media Web site, 48
wired modems, 8, 11–16, 63–64
wireless modems, 9–10, 17, 64

• *Z* •

ZIOGolf, 72

Installation Instructions

*T*he *Pocket PC StarterPak For Dummies* CD offers valuable applications and information that you won't want to miss. To install the items from the CD to your hard drive, follow these steps:

1. **Insert the CD into your computer's CD-ROM drive.**

   Sit back and relax as the CD starts itself.

2. **Look for an application or file that interests you and click on the application or file name.**

   You're taken to a screen that gives you a bit more detail about what the application does or what information the file contains. If you want to install the application, go to Step 4. Otherwise, click the Back button to return to the main menu. *Note:* If you click Exit, the CD program will close. To start the CD again, double-click on your CD drive.

3. **Make sure that your Pocket PC is connected to your desktop PC.**

4. **Click Install to download the program from your desktop PC to your Pocket PC.**

   After you install the programs you want, you can eject the CD. Carefully place it back in the plastic jacket of the book for safekeeping.

 If you have any difficulty downloading the programs from the CD to your Pocket PC, refer to the manual that came with your Pocket PC.

www.pocketpc.com

Get the most from your **Pocket PC**

Find...

- **Downloads**
- **Tips and Tricks**
- **Links to Music and Books**
- **Pocket PC PocketPaks**
- **Gateway to Everything Pocket PC**

With **pocketpc.com** you're only a click away from time-saving tips and easy, step-by-step guides on everything from the essentials to the extras. Always chock-full of informative articles with the latest software and peripheral news, and thousands of add-ons — all written by leading Pocket PC enthusiasts. **pocketpc.com** is your connection to the universe of great stuff on the Web for your Pocket PC. Come see the world of possibilities for yourself.

pocketpc.com. Start here. Do more.

Where do you want to go today?®

PocketPaks!

Smart solutions and cool gear for Pocket PCs

Targus™

Stowaway Keyboard PocketPak

Travel light. Don't let those cramped airplane trays keep you from doing your work. Just connect your Pocket PC to the Targus Stowaway Keyboard PocketPak and work in comfort.

Socket™

Mobile Email PocketPak

Ring it up. Connect your Pocket PC to most popular mobile phones for wireless Web browsing or to access your corporate network when you're away from the office. The Socket Mobile Email PocketPak also includes support for AOL and MSN clients.

Pretec™

CompactModem PocketPak

Keep up the good work. Dial into the Web or your corporate Intranet with a Pocket PC and a Pretec CompactModem PocketPak. Now it's easy to stay connected and be productive wherever you are.

Find out more about all the PocketPaks
- Connectivity • Communication • Entertainment
- Travel • Navigation • Training • Accessories
- Memory/Storage • Financial Management

Pocket PC

Learn more at www.pocketpc.com

© 2000 Microsoft Corporation. All rights reserved.
Microsoft, the Windows logo and Where do you want to go today? are either registered trademarks or trademarks of Microsoft Corporation in the US and/or other countries.

Microsoft®
Where do you want to go today?®

Get your personal copy of *Pocket PCs For Dummies*®.
Look for it wherever books are sold or visit
dummies.com.

ISBN 0-7645-0834-2   Retail Price $21.99

Dummies Books™
Bestsellers on Every Topic!

GENERAL INTEREST TITLES

BUSINESS & PERSONAL FINANCE

Accounting For Dummies®	John A. Tracy, CPA	0-7645-5014-4	$19.99 US/$27.99 CAN
Business Plans For Dummies®	Paul Tiffany, Ph.D. & Steven D. Peterson, Ph.D.	1-56884-868-4	$19.99 US/$27.99 CAN
Business Writing For Dummies®	Sheryl Lindsell-Roberts	0-7645-5134-5	$16.99 US/$27.99 CAN
Consulting For Dummies®	Bob Nelson & Peter Economy	0-7645-5034-9	$19.99 US/$27.99 CAN
Customer Service For Dummies®, 2nd Edition	Karen Leland & Keith Bailey	0-7645-5209-0	$19.99 US/$27.99 CAN
Franchising For Dummies®	Dave Thomas & Michael Seid	0-7645-5160-4	$19.99 US/$27.99 CAN
Getting Results For Dummies®	Mark H. McCormack	0-7645-5205-8	$19.99 US/$27.99 CAN
Home Buying For Dummies®	Eric Tyson, MBA & Ray Brown	1-56884-385-2	$16.99 US/$24.99 CAN
House Selling For Dummies®	Eric Tyson, MBA & Ray Brown	0-7645-5038-1	$16.99 US/$24.99 CAN
Human Resources Kit For Dummies®	Max Messmer	0-7645-5131-0	$19.99 US/$27.99 CAN
Investing For Dummies®, 2nd Edition	Eric Tyson, MBA	0-7645-5162-0	$19.99 US/$27.99 CAN
Law For Dummies®	John Ventura	1-56884-860-9	$19.99 US/$27.99 CAN
Leadership For Dummies®	Marshall Loeb & Steven Kindel	0-7645-5176-0	$19.99 US/$27.99 CAN
Managing For Dummies®	Bob Nelson & Peter Economy	1-56884-858-7	$19.99 US/$27.99 CAN
Marketing For Dummies®	Alexander Hiam	1-56884-699-1	$19.99 US/$27.99 CAN
Mutual Funds For Dummies®, 2nd Edition	Eric Tyson, MBA	0-7645-5112-4	$19.99 US/$27.99 CAN
Negotiating For Dummies®	Michael C. Donaldson & Mimi Donaldson	1-56884-867-6	$19.99 US/$27.99 CAN
Personal Finance For Dummies®, 3rd Edition	Eric Tyson, MBA	0-7645-5231-7	$19.99 US/$27.99 CAN
Personal Finance For Dummies® For Canadians, 2nd Edition	Eric Tyson, MBA & Tony Martin	0-7645-5123-X	$19.99 US/$27.99 CAN
Public Speaking For Dummies®	Malcolm Kushner	0-7645-5159-0	$16.99 US/$24.99 CAN
Sales Closing For Dummies®	Tom Hopkins	0-7645-5063-2	$14.99 US/$21.99 CAN
Sales Prospecting For Dummies®	Tom Hopkins	0-7645-5066-7	$14.99 US/$21.99 CAN
Selling For Dummies®	Tom Hopkins	1-56884-389-5	$16.99 US/$24.99 CAN
Small Business For Dummies®	Eric Tyson, MBA & Jim Schell	0-7645-5094-2	$19.99 US/$27.99 CAN
Small Business Kit For Dummies®	Richard D. Harroch	0-7645-5093-4	$24.99 US/$34.99 CAN
Taxes 2001 For Dummies®	Eric Tyson & David J. Silverman	0-7645-5306-2	$15.99 US/$23.99 CAN
Time Management For Dummies®, 2nd Edition	Jeffrey J. Mayer	0-7645-5145-0	$19.99 US/$27.99 CAN
Writing Business Letters For Dummies®	Sheryl Lindsell-Roberts	0-7645-5207-4	$16.99 US/$24.99 CAN

TECHNOLOGY TITLES

INTERNET/ONLINE

America Online® For Dummies®, 6th Edition	John Kaufeld	0-7645-0670-6	$19.99 US/$27.99 CAN
Banking Online For Dummies®	Paul Murphy	0-7645-0458-4	$24.99 US/$34.99 CAN
eBay® For Dummies®, 2nd Edition	Marcia Collier, Roland Woerner, & Stephanie Becker	0-7645-0761-3	$19.99 US/$27.99 CAN
E-Mail For Dummies®, 2nd Edition	John R. Levine, Carol Baroudi, & Arnold Reinhold	0-7645-0131-3	$24.99 US/$34.99 CAN
Genealogy Online For Dummies®, 2nd Edition	Matthew L. Helm & April Leah Helm	0-7645-0543-2	$24.99 US/$34.99 CAN
Internet Directory For Dummies®, 3rd Edition	Brad Hill	0-7645-0558-2	$24.99 US/$34.99 CAN
Internet Auctions For Dummies®	Greg Holden	0-7645-0578-9	$24.99 US/$34.99 CAN
Internet Explorer 5.5 For Windows® For Dummies®	Doug Lowe	0-7645-0738-9	$19.99 US/$28.99 CAN
Researching Online For Dummies®, 2nd Edition	Mary Ellen Bates & Reva Basch	0-7645-0546-7	$24.99 US/$34.99 CAN
Job Searching Online For Dummies®, 2nd Edition	Pam Dixon	0-7645-0673-0	$24.99 US/$34.99 CAN
Investing Online For Dummies®, 3rd Edition	Kathleen Sindell, Ph.D.	0-7645-0725-7	$24.99 US/$34.99 CAN
Travel Planning Online For Dummies®, 2nd Edition	Noah Vadnai	0-7645-0438-X	$24.99 US/$34.99 CAN
Internet Searching For Dummies®	Brad Hill	0-7645-0478-9	$24.99 US/$34.99 CAN
Yahoo!® For Dummies®, 2nd Edition	Brad Hill	0-7645-0762-1	$19.99 US/$27.99 CAN
The Internet For Dummies®, 7th Edition	John R. Levine, Carol Baroudi, & Arnold Reinhold	0-7645-0674-9	$19.99 US/$27.99 CAN

SUITES

Microsoft® Office 2000 For Windows® For Dummies®	Wallace Wang & Roger C. Parker	0-7645-0452-5	$19.99 US/$27.99 CAN
Microsoft® Office 2000 For Windows® For Dummies® Quick Reference	Doug Lowe & Bjoern Hartsfvang	0-7645-0453-3	$12.99 US/$17.99 CAN
Microsoft® Office 97 For Windows® For Dummies®	Wallace Wang & Roger C. Parker	0-7645-0050-3	$19.99 US/$27.99 CAN
Microsoft® Office 97 For Windows® For Dummies® Quick Reference	Doug Lowe	0-7645-0062-7	$12.99 US/$17.99 CAN